W9-BLO-961

Living with Big Cats

The Story of Jungle Larry,
Safari Jane,
and
David Tetzlaff

Living with Big Cats

The Story of Jungle Larry, Safari Jane, and David Tetzlaff

Sharon Rendell
with foreword by James Clubb

IZS Books

Manufactured in the United States of America
Library of Congress Card Catalog Number: 94-31632
ISBN: 0-9642604-0-9
Cover design: Lightbourne Images
Cover photo: GeorGeo's Photography

Library of Congress Cataloging-in-Publication Data

Rendell, Sharon, 1954-
    Living with big cats : the story of Jungle Larry, Safari Jane, and
    David Tetzlaff / Sharon Rendell ; with a foreword by James Clubb.
        p.   cm.
    Includes bibliographical references (p.   ).
    ISBN 0-9642604-0-9 : $11.95
    1. Tetzlaff, David, 1962- --Juvenile literature.   2. Animal
trainers--United States--Biography--Juvenile literature.   3. Lions-
-Training--United States--Juvenile literature.   4. Tigers--Training-
-United States--Juvenile literature.   5. Jungle Larry--Juvenile
literature.   6. Safari Jane--Juvenile literature.   7. Zoos--United
States--Juvenile literature.   [1. Tetzlaff, David, 1962-   .
2.   Jungle Larry.   3. Safari Jane.   4. Animal trainers.]   I. Title.
GV1811.T48R45   1994
636.088'8--dc20
    [B]   94-31632
                                                                          CIP
                                                                          AC

IZS Books
a publication of the International Zoological Society, Inc.
Naples, Florida
in association with Tabby House
Charlotte Harbor, Florida

To *my family, Larry and Paul,*
the Tetzlaffs,
and to Centaine and her friends.

Contents

Foreword

WHEN I FIRST met David Tetzlaff in 1987 at Jungle Larry's in Naples, Florida, I was over from the United Kingdom supervising the rehearsals for my group of fourteen lions that were to make their debut with the new edition of Ringling Brothers "Greatest Show on Earth." Another trainer had told me about Jungle Larry's and a young man there who had trained a large group of leopards. Leopard acts are unusual and I myself own the only such act in Europe. I decided to drive down to Naples one morning to take a look. On arrival I found to my disappointment that the park was closed, but when I introduced myself I was greeted in very grand style.

Here was a wild-animal trainer unlike the old-fashioned, brusque stereotype. David appeared modest of his own achievements, gangling in manner, apparently shy, yet articulate and intelligent.

I was even more impressed when I later witnessed David at work with his big cats. The audiences were enthusiastic in their response to his performances, but only someone who has seen the great trainers in the world or who has worked with animals themselves could really appreciate how impressive, hazardous and complicated the routine is that David has perfected with his leopards and black panthers. His rapport with his working animals and his care and professional pride in the zoo park and with its inhabitants are highly impressive.

Friends across the sea—David and Jim Clubb (right).

Since that first meeting I have come to know David well as a friend and a fellow traveler touring the great circuses of Europe with me, and once giving me a hair-raising drive through the hairpin bends of the Swiss Alps! He also surprises the artists and trainers he meets with his Florida style of dress, wearing shorts and no socks, even in the cold winters in England.

We have worked together and I have helped him train at Jungle Larry's with his own animals. He has looked after many cubs born to tigers, leopards, and hyenas from my own groups on tour with Ringling Bros., and he and his staff always care for them in an exemplary way.

JAMES CLUBB,
Owner, Clubb-Chipperfield Limited

Preface

The fall after I was hired, David's mother, Nancy Jane, gave an employee dinner at a very nice restaurant here in town. I was seated at another table but couldn't help noticing that as soon as Nancy entered the room, David immediately stood up. I can't say why that impressed me so much, but it did. I suppose it is because most young men today have lost their courtesy and David is, above all else, a gentleman. Nothing feigned or phony, he is quite simply a gentleman and carries it off with the same grace he displays when he does his tiger act.

—Penny Hollon, animal caretaker

ONE WARM DECEMBER afternoon, I watched spellbound as David Tetzlaff trained leopards. Although I had seen the leopard act earlier that day, I was still fascinated to see David's rapport with the animals. How could he have such a close relationship with majestic wild animals? His big cats even want to be petted before leaving the arena, yet they are not placid. I knew that at times they have spats, much like domestic cats in a family living room. When I talked with David later and he showed and told me how he trained tigers and leopards to perform on request, I told him I wanted to write a book to share his story.

Aside from telling David's story, I had several other reasons for writing *Living with Big Cats:* personally, I am enchanted by the big cats—looking into their soulful eyes, watching their soft fur ripple as they move. I am also concerned that the big cats are in danger of extinction, and greater awareness of the facts may avoid that; I am impressed with the Tetzlaff family's values that are evident in their work and park (park cleanliness, the outgoing, cheerful personnel); and I love the subtropical climate and vegetation at Jungle Larry's at Caribbean Gardens in Naples, Florida.

Even in the parking area, there are red and purple leaves of ten-foot tall crotons, delicate pink flowers of the powder puff bush and red elongated flowers of the bottlebrush tree. The fragrance of the orchid trees' purple flowers and the cascading magenta bougainvillea suggest a tropical island. The blue sky is so dazzling that it hurts the eyes; the shady deep green foliage of the jungle provides a restful contrast. Jungle Larry's Zoological Park is the largest truly tropical garden with animals in America.

My research for this book began in 1991. I looked through hundreds of photos and several scrapbooks covering the previous thirty years. I observed David's cat shows in person and on video. I visited the Tetzlaffs' second park location, Cedar Point once, and returned to the Naples site numerous times. In each park I accompanied David as he followed his daily routine. I interviewed his mother, Nancy Jane Tetzlaff-Berens, who is chief executive officer of Jungle Larry's. I also talked with some of the other renowned animal trainers, David's relatives, friends, and Jungle Larry's veterinarians and employees—in all more than thirty people.

The transcripts from these taped interviews totaled about 1,200 pages providing the basis for *Living with Big Cats.*

I deeply appreciate the eager cooperation of all sources of information: David and Nancy Jane; Jungle Larry's veterinarians; the many family members, friends, and employees of the Tetzlaffs, also the animal trainers and former zoo directors: Mike Cecere, James Clubb, Jack Hanna, Frank Thompson, Roy Wells, Pat White, and Ron Whitfield. Each person was enthusiastic and helpful, making my job easier and more fun.

When I first visited Jungle Larry's that December day, David Tetzlaff had never met me, but he took time to talk. As I got to know him better, I realized my first impressions of his strength and kindness were accurate.

During the three years we spent together on this project, I have found a friend in Nancy. Always stylish, she is quite the businesswoman—organized, pleasant, reasonable, working well with her employees and the public. She is gentle with people and animals. With me, Nancy has been sensitive, open and trusting. At times, in her soft voice, she revealed personal matters—sometimes poignant memories which were hard for her to relive.

I also became closer to the big cats. I was elated when Nancy suggested I bottle-feed a six-week-old jaguar, Maya, for a photograph for this book. Very few employees are allowed even to touch a cub. Nancy took a chunk of her busy day to photograph Maya and me. I'll never forget the feeling of holding Maya—and the surprise I felt by how strong and feisty she was. After I fed the hungry cub with the formula in the baby bottle, I thought I could put her head on my shoulder and cuddle her. But a kitten is a kitten and after she was satisfied, Maya wanted to wiggle, squirm, and play. Nancy told me I could not let Maya touch the ground, as she had not yet had her first vaccinations (due the following Friday). So I gently but firmly held her, smiling and laughing in my delight.

In these three years of my observations of Jungle Larry's, I have witnessed a number of changes, such as the development of the safari boat ride. One change was sad: Grant Smith, head tram driver and show narrator, who lived at the Naples park, passed away September 1993 at the age of seventy. He had been a bright spot at Jungle Larry's for four years—easy to like, joyful, exuberant, and full of life.

Many of today's prominent animal trainers, such as Wade Burck, Roy Wells, Pat White, and Mike Cecere, began their careers at Jungle Larry's. Excerpts from my interviews with trainers and other people in the field appear throughout this book. Mike Cecere currently manages the Double M Ranch Historical American Circus in Hastings, New York. I agree with his comment, "[David is] a very intelligent person. With his dedication there is no stopping him!"

SHARON RENDELL
Urbana, Illinois

PART ONE

David trains as it
should be done...
He makes the most
difficult tricks look easy.
—Mike Cecere, trainer

1

Tangling with Tigers

Every time you go in the ring, you have to treat it like the first time, because the animals all have their teeth, claws, and instincts. A complacent cat can do as much damage as an aggressive one. —David Tetzlaff

A TENNIS PLAYER or an investment banker can afford an occasional error, but an animal trainer cannot. Wild animals are dangerous. Just one mistake could be fatal for David Tetzlaff, a world-renowned animal trainer based at Jungle Larry's Caribbean Gardens in Naples, Florida. By the time David was thirty years old, he was a thirteen-year veteran of the big cat arena. With David's talent, his performances are considered on par with the big cat acts of such famous trainers as Clyde Beatty, Charly Baumann, and Gunther Gebel-Williams.

David, the older son of the late "Jungle Larry" Tetzlaff, has been showcased in *People* magazine and many newspapers, and has appeared on numerous TV shows. In 1992, a TV crew flew to Florida from Japan to feature him in a one-hour documentary about animal training in America. He also has written critiques of other trainers' acts in trade publications, such as *King Pole,* published in England, and *Circus Report,* published in the United

States, and his editorial comments about cat acts and trainers have been published in many newspapers in the United States.

During one training session I observed, David stood alone in the forty-foot-wide performance arena with three full-grown trained Bengal tigers. He was introducing three sixteen-month-old "cubs" to the established troupe. David—six feet four-inches and built like a basketball player—was dwarfed by the massive orange and black tigers. I was impressed by their relative size.

Many people have the misconception that the lion ("king of the jungle") is the largest cat. Lions seem larger than others because of their huge head and mane, but the tiger is actually bigger. Lions can weigh 320 to 500 pounds, but the male tigers in David's act weigh 550 pounds. Massive as they are, they move their bulk fluidly, their powerful muscles allowing them to jump from one pedestal to another as easily as a house cat springs from a footstool to a couch.

1.1 David performing a six-tiger sit-up at Cedar Point.

It's customary for an animal trainer to have a helper called a back-up or spotter. From the safety cage (a metal and wire enclosure just behind the performance ring), the back-up watches the animals in the ring. Training sessions don't begin in the performance arena until after the back-up hangs signs which read:

"Training session in progress. Feel free to quietly observe." If the back-up sees a cat's ears go flat, eyes glaze, or anything else indicating a dissatisfied cat, he alerts the trainer. The back-up goes into the arena only when invited during the training sessions, and during a performance only if the trainer is injured badly enough to be on the floor. It's important that the animals perceive the trainer as the only one in charge.

Art Kozlik, former back-up for David and longtime manager of Jungle Larry's at Cedar Point Park in Sandusky, Ohio, told me, "I think the most dangerous thing for an animal trainer is that you don't know for sure if your back-up will come in and help you if something should happen. One trainer had the same back-up for years," he said. "When he got into trouble, the back-up got scared and wouldn't come into the arena and help."

Art smiled and raised his eyebrows, "You don't know yourself until an emergency happens. When the time comes, would you go in?"

On this warm November day, because of the possiblility of problems, David's back-up, Jeff, was in the ring. He looked like a president's bodyguard, eyes sweeping back and forth as he stood ready to help. David worked with the tigers while Jeff held a throat fork. This tool is used defensively if a cat attacks the trainer or it may be used to break up a fight between cats. The trainer or back-up puts the Y-shaped end of the stick at the animal's throat, forcing him to release his grip. Or it may be used to keep an aggressive cat at bay. A throat fork is far more effective than a stick.

I sat taking notes in the bleachers. Suddenly, a problem. David had called five tigers, one by one into the center of the ring to lie down, side by side, with paws outstretched. One trained female, Delhi, lay next to a young male, Shikar. Suddenly, in the time it took for me to glance down at my notes, the scene changed. Delhi yowled, growled, turned to her side, opened her vast mouth, and grabbed Shikar by the back of the neck. Shikar's wide eyes showed his fear and confusion.

David yelled at Delhi, "Stop it!" while he and Jeff tried the throat fork to release her hold. Fortunately, she did not bite hard enough to hurt Shikar, and she let go of him after about thirty seconds, leaving the young male unhurt.

Later, when I asked David about Delhi's rough behavior toward another troupe member, he told me it's fairly unusual for something like that to happen. When I commented that it was scary for those who were watching, he replied, "It was scarier for us! We were in there. It's nothing looking from the outside. Get inside, then you find out what fear is. All they have to do is grab you once, shake you and you're done for. The only way to survive is to always pay attention and react quickly with no hesitation. That's when trainers get hurt, or animals get hurt—if they hesitate or don't pay attention."

Fortunately, in contrast to this incident, most training sessions go so smoothly that sometimes people passing the arena have mistaken them for actual shows—without narration.

Despite the unpredictability of these huge animals, David loves his work.

Teen-age Trainer

David began in the animal business at age fourteen when he first presented chimp and elephant acts at Jungle Larry's. In 1980 when he was eighteen years old, he began training leopards, and by the late eighties was considered one of the world's top leopard trainers. Ready for a new challenge, in 1991 he began developing a tiger act. He started with Prince, an eight-year-old tiger he had hand-raised from birth—bottle-feeding Prince and letting him sleep with him on his queen-size bed.

1.2 David (left) and Tim, with family dogs and tiger cub, 1982.

It is easy to see that David is sensitive to the individual differences in his cats. "You've got to find ways to make them all enjoy it. So you don't push the cats to do something they're not going to like. For instance, I stopped training Nirvana to roll over. She just didn't like it. She wasn't doing that well, so I stopped. Then again, she's a good cat for a shoulder stand." (In this behavior, or trick, the tiger stands on her hind legs, puts her front paws on David's shoulders and looks him in the eyes. The entire trick lasts about thirty seconds.)

In the early 1990s David had a of lot responsibility as Jungle Larry's only big cat trainer. He told me that over the years he's missed only five days' work. "And that was when I was hurt and couldn't use my arm. Otherwise I've been [in the arena] with bronchitis, in stitches, [or with] my back pulled out. I can't re-

member a time I was too sick to work. Basically the few times I've gone on vacation are the only times I've missed [since he was eighteen-years old, presenting his leopard act twice daily, six days a week]."

2

The Tiger Act

In 1982 David Tetzlaff was the head animal trainer at Jungle Larry's. At twenty-two years, David was said to be the youngest trainer in the world.
—Cedar Point Amusement Park

IT'S THREE MINUTES to show time in Naples. Peppy music directs attention to the big arena. A tram-load of people disembarks after their tour of the park. More visitors are just entering the park, making the tiger show their first stop. A group of pre-schoolers and their teachers come down the path from the petting zoo and climb the bleachers where I am sitting. During the height of season, the crowd is at capacity with many people standing.

Three tigers have just entered the arena. An employee pulls a rope opening another chute and two more tigers enter. On the other side of the arena the back-up lets two more tigers in. Four tigers saunter to their pedestals and sit down. The other three walk around the arena, looking over this morning's audience before going to sit on their assigned pedestals.

The announcer begins a typical narration: "At thirty, a thirteen-year veteran of the big cat arena and one of the great trainers in the world, David Tetzlaff! [Applause] David began his career with wild animals at the age of fourteen. He has worked with a variety of animals but prefers the big cats. He began training cats in 1982 and since then he has worked with nearly forty leopards, lions, tigers, jaguars, and panthers. He is now recognized as one of the most respected trainers in his field."

2.1 In a trick rarely performed by other trainers, David is astride Prince while Bengal leaps through a hoop over their heads.

David enters the arena dressed in gray shorts, a green Jungle Larry's polo shirt, and athletic shoes. As he sets up pedestals for the first trained "behavior," he narrates his show via the microphone clipped to his shirt pocket. At David's first word, the music stops. He introduces the cats to the audience, saying their names and ages. Then he explains how Jungle Larry's treats its animals. "A couple of misconceptions people have about performing big cats: some people assume that trainers automatically declaw their animals. At Jungle Larry's we do not. Since we opened in 1969, we've trained over sixty big cats for our shows and we never found it necessary to defang or declaw any of our animals. Also people think we feed the animals before the show to make them more docile, sleepy, so they don't attack their trainer. Their stomach doesn't have much to do with their attitude. An aggressive tiger will kill you on a full stomach, so feeding them before a show doesn't matter too much. These guys perform twice a day and they'll eat after this performance. Most of these guys eat at least ten pounds of fresh beef and chicken apiece, each and every day. You'll notice I have a little bit of food with me in my small bait pouch. This is for the benefit of my three new tigers I'm putting into the show, and also if one of the older guys performs exceptionally well, I'll give him a reward."

In his famous tiger act, David uses upbeat instrumental music as a background for the big cats' performance.

The first trick is one rarely attempted by other trainers. Prince, a huge male, stands with his front feet on one three-foot-high pedestal with his back feet on an identical pedestal. David climbs up to sit on Prince's back as if riding a horse. While he sits on Prince, another tiger, Bengal, bounds from one side of the arena, jumps briefly on a pedestal to their right, then leaps in a high arc over David and Price through a hoop that David holds high over his head. The crowd is in awe. But there is much more.

2.2 David circles Prince and Bengal as they turn on their spindles.

On a given day, David's act may include various combinations of the following tricks or behaviors: Six tigers sit on pedestals in "pyramid" form, then move to sit up on their hind legs. Then, three tigers place forepaws on spindles (pedestals with movable tops), then walk in a circle around the spindle. Soon all tigers sit on hind legs and raise their paws. To the audience's amazement, Centaine, who weighs 350 pounds, walks over Bengal and sits up, then raises her front legs. It's an elephant trick that David has taught the tigers. Alone, Centaine pirouettes on her hind legs. As the act continues all tigers lie down touching lengthwise, then all sit up together. Bengal then walks backward on his hind legs.

Between the tricks, David talks about conservation. "Right now there are about four thousand tigers left in the countries of India, Bangladesh, and Nepal. A pretty small number. Ninety years ago there were 40,000 tigers out there. You can see what the encroachment of man and loss of habitat has done to one species alone. It sounds ironic, but there are about four thousand Bengal tigers in captivity. A lot of people wonder: if there are so many in captivity, why don't they release them into the wild? The problem is, there's not much wild to go back to. Take India, for example. They're developing the country. Ninety-seven percent of the land is set aside for people; three percent for animals. A lot of people over there don't care about the animals and are more or less concerned with developing for the money. So zoos may be the only way to preserve endangered species."

While David sets up various height pedestals for the pyramid, he explains different aspects of training. "I start training tigers when they're eleven months old. They all learn at different rates, just like children do in a classroom. The rate of learning depends on the individual. It takes from six to eighteen months to get ready for a show. Bengal was trained in six or seven months; Prince in fourteen months. The training is step-by-step and looks nothing like the finished product. The nine-foot jumps begin by enticing the tigers with meat to step across the pedestals, so they can be sure of a solid landing."

When the props are in place and David stops talking, the music resumes and David cues the tigers' next trick. The words "trick" and "behavior" are often used interchangeably, but, historically, "trick" characterizes trained actions—things that the animals would never do on their own—such as an elephant playing a harmonica. Many modern trainers now showcase the animals' natural abilities, such as jumping or walking on parallel ropes eight feet above the ground. David often uses the word "behavior" to describe these natural abilities that he shapes into an act.

Before the hind-leg walk, David elaborates: "Standing on hind legs is a natural thing for tigers. It's one way they play as cubs and also fight as adults. In the wild, both animals rear up like ponies, which puts them on equal terms, then one tries to knock the other to the ground. It's a natural aggressive behavior that we're turning into a non-aggressive demonstration for the show."

David explains the tiger's noises. "A tiger's 'chuffle' is a friendly greeting. He does it by blowing air through his lips. The sound doesn't come out of the throat like it does with a house cat." One of the tigers interrupts with a "ROARRRRR," startling the audience. David smiles, "Prince is always mouthing off, belligerent. Everyone asks if he's having a bad day. No, he's always like that. So at least I have no surprises.

2.3 David fine-tuning the six-tiger sit-up in practice, preparing for the public appearance.

"The females usually weigh 350-400 pounds. This one, Delhi, born in 1987, is a golden tiger. She looks like a house cat on steroids. The first golden tiger was born in captivity in 1976 and only fifteen like her exist in the entire world. This makes the golden tiger even more rare than the white tiger. Delhi has a recessive gene for white tigers. Our youngest male also has a recessive white gene, so if these two mate, they have a one in four chance of producing a white tiger."

After the act the announcer tells the audience: "You'll note that when the tigers exit the arena, they leave in a specific order, as tigers by nature are solitary, very independent animals. Tigers live in designated groups and they can all be together only under David's supervision."

David usually pets the last two tigers while they await their turn to exit. They lean into his caressing hand, and in the thirty-some performances I witnessed, the crowd never failed to give a satisfied "awwww." Petting a tiger may look like petting a big kitty but it is the relationship between the trainer and cat that allows such closeness. Many trainers are not able to stand that close to the animals, nor do they seem as affectionate toward their crew of cats.

After the performance when the animals are out of the arena, David walks to the front to answer questions from the audience:

Q: "Why do you feed the animals yourself?"

A: "Younger animals like a particular person to bring the food. You build a relationship with them that way. When a cat is older, the animal just wants food and wants it NOW."

Q: "What is your performance schedule?"

A: "We get a day off in the winter and usually in the summer we work daily, but it's only two shows a day. We feel wild animals should only perform twice daily. It keeps them occupied without overworking them. It's the same with bird shows: four or five times a day is too much work for the birds. We do ours once or twice a day."

Q: "Where were your animals born?"

A: "All my leopards were born here. A couple of the tigers were born here. The rest were born at the trainer Josip Marcan's place. I bought them as five- to nine-month-old cubs and I finished raising and training them here."

Audiences inevitably ask about the danger David is in and if he's been injured. David doesn't volunteer details unless asked.

Q: "Have you been hurt by a cat?"

A: "Sometimes. You can't be a race-car driver and not expect to hit the wall once in a while. Usually you have to blame yourself, not the animal. A lot of it is accidental. The worst I got hurt was breaking up a fight between two tigers. The tigers didn't get hurt, I did. When animals get into it, it's your job to stop it, because they could kill each other right in front of you." Another day his answer to this question is a simple, "I've had six stitch jobs."

Naturally, each audience tends to be curious about the same topics. I asked David if he tires of answering the same questions. He looked surprised at my question and replied, "No, be-

cause it's a different crowd every time. It'd be like saying you get tired of the show. Each time it's a whole new experience. Each time presenting an act, you have to bring the cats and crowds together to make everything work."

3

From Novice to Expert Trainer

[At] twenty-nine [I was] a dinosaur. Not many people have come up behind me in the last ten years. Back then I was one of the youngest trainers in the United States and a decade later, I still am. —David Tetzlaff

WITH NO VOCATIONAL schools teaching how to train animals, the only way to learn is by working closely with a trainer. Larry Tetzlaff taught more than fifty people and many of them became outstanding zoo directors and curators. Oddly enough, he did not officially train his son. Starting when he was very young, David learned the basics by watching his father. He observed Larry train and perform, learned how to take care of the animals and how to observe their behavior—for example, to watch their eyes and ears for signs of alarm or fear.

David presented (performed an act with) elephants and chimps when he was barely a teen. By the time he graduated from high school in 1981, he had begun training his first four leopards for a complicated act that eventually grew to seventeen leopards. Then in 1982, between performances, David began training another cat act using two Bengal tigers and an African lioness.

Leopards are considered by most to be more difficult to train than either lions or tigers. But, after his success with leopards,

3.1 David's pleasure is obvious as he plays with Jet and Honey, three-month-old leopard cubs.

David wanted a new challenge. Because Americans think that bigger cats are better to watch, David developed a tiger act in 1990. He started the act with the two Bengal tigers from his tiger-and-lioness act and a new adult golden tiger. In 1992 David added three young tigers to the established act.

Long before David's fame with leopards, he began by presenting other animals. Every trainer wants to make it look like he's the best—whatever animal he trains is the best species to train, David told me. So there is a lot of pride in putting together an act. David's first experience in the ring was at Jungle Larry's park when he was thirteen. He helped hold two elephants in place while a leopard jumped from one elephant's back to the other's for their German trainer, Dieter Wichert. From Roy Wells, who was then the park's trainer, David learned more about elephants. Before David began training his own animals, he learned how to present three four-year-old African elephants that Wells had trained. The elephants must have liked David, because as Jungle Larry said, African elephants are so high-strung that they have to fall in love with the trainer or they won't perform. Although an Asian elephant usually will perform if a trainer nudges him with a stick, Africans are so stubborn that they'll only perform to please themselves. Despite his experience presenting elephants, David is quick to say he is not an elephant trainer.

3.2 David encourages an adult leopard to perform the difficult fire jump.

David presented chimpanzees between elephant performances from 1981 to 1987. In one trick a baby elephant with a chimp riding on his back would first balance on his hind legs, then the elephant would walk a plank. In that act the chimps also walked on stilts, roller skated, somersaulted, and bicycled. The most unusual thing the chimps did was to walk a tightrope blindfolded, one chimp facing forward, one backward.

As we were talking, David was supervising three leopards in the arena. He sat on a show pedestal and ate the ham sandwich he made hours earlier. I sat on the cement on the other side of the bars with my tape recorder. David told me that in 1982 he was training a chimp named JJ. "I built on what other trainers had done. JJ had been taught to walk on four-foot-high stilts. I put him on eight-foot-high stilts. It was just a matter of building him up over a few weeks. He knew how to roller skate. I taught him to high jump on roller skates. He used to roll a ball. I taught him to roll a ball on one foot, a trick I hadn't seen before."

3.3 David at fourteen, in one of his early performances with a young African elephant.

Yet David doesn't want to be called a chimp trainer either. His mother thinks his unease with chimps may be because of an accident when he was fourteen years old. A chimp, frightened by a disturbance in the audience, jumped off the elephant it was riding, biting David on the way down. Art Kozlik, who has known David for many years, said David has a good rapport with every species except chimps.

When David and I talked about working with other species he said, "I'm not going to put down the courage of a bear trainer or elephant trainer or chimp trainer. In fact, probably more people have been bitten by chimpanzees than cats. I guess chimps are one of the smartest animals, but I think they don't have a lick of common sense. Chimps love to make trouble just to get your attention. Partially what drove me up a wall working with chimps is they don't care about irritating you as long as you look at them."

David does not like to see chimps dressed up in acts, doing "cute" tricks mimicking people. He likes bringing out an animal's natural beauty and grace, as he does with his cat acts. "I'm just a cat man—it's all I'll ever care so deeply about."

David Begins to Train Leopards

David's career was shaped by various people. Aside from watching his father at work, he read about other trainers and watched

3.4 A rare accomplishment—getting five chimpanzees and an African elephant to accept each other for an act.

circus acts. At an early age, he was impressed with what he read about Alfred Court, one of his all-time favorite trainers. As we talked about some of his early influences, David played with a seven-month-old leopard which he named after Court. "Mr. Court died in the late 1970s when he was over ninety. He was a genius. Most people can't touch his acts today, fifty years later.

"He came over here from Europe in the early 1940s with sixty wild animals, three rings, and three or four trainers. Clyde Beatty was here with a blank gun and chair, but Court came over here with a little whip and did it differently," David told me.

Some of Court's most impressive work was a mixed act with six black leopards, two jaguars, two snow leopards, four pumas and ten Indian and African leopards—most of which were captured wild, because few were hand-raised back in the 1940s. An innovative act of the early 1940s, "The Beauties and the Beasts," featured one dozen leopards and one dozen girls. Court trained the animals, then had male assistants dressed in pink leotards stand by each animal. Finally, one by one, twelve lovely young women in leotards replaced the assistants.

David read that Court said that "caution is more valuable than courage." David added, "The best defense is knowledge—not only of the species, but of the individual animal's personality." Court didn't try to force a cat to do a trick it did not like. With a little extra effort, the trainer can find a set of behaviors a particular cat will enjoy. David, like Court, found that this extra effort is one of the ingredients to success. David never saw Court perform his acts.

A circus buff from the time he was thirteen, he never missed a chance to learn by watching performers. Of the modern famous circus trainers, David thinks most highly of Ringling's German-born Gunther Gebel-Williams. Although David does not know Gebel-Williams personally, he has been greatly influenced by his energy and his rapport with leopards.

3.5 David catching Ebony, a black leopard that is trained to leap from a pedestal into his arms.

David said, "When I was seventeen, during my first three training years, I was on my own. I saw Wichert train a couple of leopards at Jungle Larry's when I was still in high school. So I took what I saw him do and what I saw in circuses, and formulated my own way of doing it. A few years later I finally got to see some other trainers practice—Ron Whitfield, in Redwood City, California, John Cox, John Campolongo, and James Clubb in England. I took the best of what I liked and added to it."

David received encouragement from both friends and family. From 1985 to 1992 he was married to Melinda ("Mindy") Howman and the couple had a son, Sasha, in 1988. During that time Mindy was both confidante and good critic. Because she often watched him train the leopards, she was usually the first person he asked: "How did it go? What did you think of it?" Mindy and David remain friends today.

3.6 David and Mindy with two of their friends in 1986.

Pat White worked four lions for Jungle Larry's in the 1970s. David, then a young teen presenting animals but not yet training any, observed the way Pat built on the training Roy Wells had begun with the lions. David told me that his career with lions was influenced by Pat's determination and feistiness, attributes that help in training animals. "Pat does what she feels is right for her animals and I always try to do this too."

The Leopard Act

By the time David was eighteen he knew big cat training would be his life's work. Until then he was planning to earn a college zoology degree. Larry and Nancy had been in favor of the zoology career, but changed their minds during the spring of David's senior high school year when his dad took him to visit a school that offered a two-year program in animal husbandry. David told me, "We looked around there and when we walked out Dad said [based on David's experience and knowledge], 'You could teach here.'

"In March 1981 the first four leopards were old enough to start training. I asked Dad if I could do it and he said 'Go ahead and try.' Once I started training, I never thought about college again. And once my parents saw I enjoyed it and was good at it, they never bothered me about college again." However, David is an avid reader and continues to consume books on all aspects of animal life, training, and handling.

3.7 David holds the hoop while a leopard sails through.

David has presented the leopard act since 1984, starting with his troupe of four leopards. He kept adding animals until eventually he was able to work seventeen leopards at one time—the third largest act in history, after Gunther Gebel-Williams and Alfred Court. David's leopards could perform twenty-two tricks, several of them distinctive. A well-known circus offered David $50,000 for his leopard act so one of their people could present it. He refused.

"Leopards are so intelligent and clever. It's the beauty of it and the undoing of it. The smarter an animal is the more ways it thinks of to outsmart you and try to be two or three steps ahead of you, which I like," David said. He's trained about twenty in the last ten years and "every one was a devil with something up his sleeve. You have to laugh sometimes—the sneaky things they think up. It makes them harder to train than lions or tigers."

Lions may maul and leave. However, if a leopard attacks a man, it's to kill. In David's act he hand-feeds treats to leopards to keep them attentive and happy. David used mostly female leopards and only four males in the act. Males lend stability to the act. "Females stir up trouble—but nothing that positive, stern commands can't correct."

David Learned from Experts

Mike Cecere, now manager of a circus in New York, trained lions and tigers at Jungle Larry's from 1979 to 1982. During his more than twenty-year career, he has trained many exotic animals, including, camels, llamas, elephants, chimps, and bears as well as the big cats.

I telephoned Cecere because he had coached David in the basics of seat-training leopards in the spring of 1981. He spoke enthusiastically. "[David] has a gift for working with animals. I spotted it right away when I first came to work there." Cecere told me that even though his pupil was the park owner's son, David had started at the bottom and worked his way up. "His devotion and work ethic put him on the fast track, for sure, but he worked hard for his success."

David smiled as he recalled what he'd learned from Mike and added that he and Mike still phone each other periodically. "When Mike Cecere quit Jungle Larry's in 1982 to perform in a circus in South America, he complimented me: 'You got better even faster than I thought you would.'

"The main thing I learned from Mike was to exercise your animals between the shows. Don't leave them in the cage. He used to go into the arena and sit and have lunch with his lions, so that's where I got that idea. Mike kept his cages spotlessly clean and that influenced me too. Little things, like washing the blood away when they're done eating so you don't have ants in the cage. Mike had such drive—he was an example of dedication overkill, working for two years with no day off."

During the summer of 1984, in Ohio, David introduced an act of two tigers and a lion. Those appearances were called "sched-

3.8 Mike Cecere performing with the Jungle Larry tigers at Cedar Point.

uled practice sessions." The site, in keeping with the Tetzlaff's
Florida location, was decorated with purple, pink, and red bro-
meliads, a type of orchid that had been brought north and arranged on the native trees of Ohio. The audience enjoyed the acts
in seventy-degree weather with a breeze off Lake Erie. To the
300 to 400 people watching him train, the performance appeared
part training, part act. As David improved, he described his training work as an act.

Looking back to that time when he was nineteen years old,
David said his act wasn't spectacular. In fact, when he first began seat training leopards he had some disconcerting experiences.
As a guide at Jungle Larry's, Paul Pifer, watched David learning.
From Paul's account, when David first started training leopards,
he was very frustrated for a number of months. "In one corner
he'd have Larry yelling to him and in another corner he'd have
Mike Cecere instructing him, and occasionally Nancy would yell
advice from another corner. David would get frustrated, throw a
pedestal across the arena, and run out, then would come back
when everybody had left and do it his way. [His own method]
obviously worked."

David also has a special place in his heart for two other famous trainers: Josip Marcan and James Clubb. David met Marcan
for the first time in 1983. Unfortunately, David had been recently
injured by a leopard and was unable to perform for Marcan. A
year later Marcan returned to observe David at work with his

leopards. They became friends. Marcan, a native of Yugoslavia, has trained big cats for more than thirty years and presented them around the world in the big circuses. He has bred and trained animals for the Clyde Beatty-Cole Brothers Circus since 1985. David believes that "Josip Marcan out trains everybody no matter what he does. He had a fantastic act with twelve lions before he began training tigers. He had a seventeen-tiger lay down and sit-up. Nobody else did that. Josip also did a liberty [without leash] waltz with tigers. I've told Jim Clubb flat out I think Josip's the best tiger trainer in the world. He has a gift for tigers like you wouldn't believe. He's probably one of my best role models."

Marcan's perseverance speaks to the perfectionist side of David. He, too, puts in whatever time it takes to make his act its best.

David was well aware of James Clubb's training achievements from reading British trade publications and had developed great respect for Clubb even before meeting him. Clubb has been in the business since first managing a zoo at age eighteen.

3.9 David learns how to work with a tiger from well-known trainer, Josip Marcan.

Here's David's story: "I first met Jim in person in December of 1987. At that time we did not open the park on Mondays. So on those days the show staff would come and care for the animals and take a half-day off, returning later to check on the animals in the late afternoon. One day we had just finished our morning chores when I got a call from Larry Allen Dean (a trainer who was working Clubb's lions), who was driving down to Naples from Ringling's winter quarters in Venice with James Clubb. I was totally floored. Jim Clubb coming here! No way!

"It turned out that Jim had been talking to Carmen Hall (who has one of the best primate acts around featuring drills, mandrills, and Gelada baboons) and they were discussing leopard acts and Carmen told Jim about my act. So needless to say I was honored that Jim Clubb would drive an hour and a half to see my act when he could have been having a barbecue with the Ringling trainers up in Venice instead.

"On that Monday when we were closed I set up the show and lined up the leopards before Jim arrived. We did the entire show for three people: Jim, Larry Dean, and my mother. It was the smallest group I had ever worked for, but it was one of the most important shows of my career because it got me Jim's respect as a trainer and that alone opened many doors that were closed to me before. Jim not only became my good friend, but he also taught me much about animals and training, and introduced me to many of the world's top trainers.

"I remember going up into the stands after the act was finished and the first thing he said to me was, 'You can have a job with me anytime.' Which, of course, was high praise from someone I had just met."

David proudly told me, "The guy's barely forty years old and he's already trained over twenty acts. I've trained twenty leopards so far, but he's trained forty. I think Jim Clubb is the best all-round animal trainer. When I first went to England in 1989, in one day he was in the ring with alligators, lions, tigers, leopards, black panthers, a jaguar, black bear, Himalayan bear, polar bears, and brown bears. He worked with ten different species in the same day. Who else does that? To be able to do that and change your attitude from one species to the next would make most trainers' heads spin. But he doesn't clean or feed the animals; everything's set up for him. The way he works is—practice, have an assistant put the animals away and get the next group of animals ready, while Jim makes his business calls. He comes back when the setup is ready in ten minutes, repeating this process all day long. I really respect Jim for that ability. Watching Jim work like this inspires me to consider training a mixed act."

Now circus people come to see David's show—Jim Clubb, Josip Marcan, Sacha Houcke, Wade Burck, Pat White, and Roy Wells. David talked to me in his Cedar Point dressing room, a small,

3.10 One of England's great trainers, Jim Clubb, with tiger and lion lay down. (photo courtesy of Jim Clubb)

simple room with an old recliner, a desk, a couch, and a roll of carpet remnant. Its walls are covered with circus posters and photos of David and his many acts. He uses it to change into his performance uniform, and for some well-deserved peace and quiet.

As with any field, David said his first few years were an important part of the learning process. "Not that the animals weren't any good; I just needed to learn more.

"I've had a lot of people watch me. You're always scared to death you'll screw up if you know they're in the audience. You want to impress them and show that you might halfway know what you're doing. I'd get beside myself if the cats screwed up in front of somebody famous, but after awhile, I had to realize, hey, their stuff messes up, too, and I've seen that happen. But if somebody only comes to see you once, you just want to shine."

David continued, "The four big leopard acts of our time, plus Alfred Court of the past, are the best ones. In the last twenty years, Dickie Chipperfield, Jr.'s, Jim Clubb's, Gunther Gebel-Williams', and mine are the leopard acts. It's really hard to say which was best, because we each had a trick or two the others didn't.

"Yet you can find similar stuff in everybody's act. One trick, of leopards crossing sticks on fire, I thought was original. Apparently that trainer saw somebody in France do it. But then, everybody comes up with a little something you might not see anywhere else. Gunther Gebel-Williams, and Charly Baumann, probably came up with the newest stuff in tiger training—like Gunther's original trick of having two tigers each hold an end of a stick that's on fire in the middle. Clubb, Chipperfield, Gebel-Williams and I all used the stepping-stone trick in our leopard acts.

"Few new acts have been started from scratch by young trainers since 1981. It takes too much time, effort and work, and the only inspiration is your own drive." David leaned back and sighed, settling into his patched recliner. "Leopards are such a touchy thing. I look back and all the things I did with leopards—I can't believe it today. I just never appreciated what I could do with those cats then; I took it for granted.

"Looking back I could never do that again. I don't have the patience. If you said to me train twelve leopards, I really couldn't do it. It's just taken so much of my energy in that direction—to get your patience extended that far for them."

Most trainers are fortunate to have one internationally impressive act. "My leopard act is something I did for so long. I proved myself. With the leopards I did six and seven rolling over. Who's done that? Gunther [Gebel-Williams] is the only one who's done that many leopards. Then you have Wade Burck and Charly Baumann, who did that many with tigers. So probably fewer than ten people ever did it with any more than five cats rolling over. It's very hard to train. But the first five leopards I broke to roll over, I used five spotted ones and it was letter perfect."

Training Lions and Tigers

When Pat White left to work for a circus, Jungle Larry presented the lion troupe she had worked with at the park. When Larry retired from the cage in 1982, David worked those lions until he trained a lion and tiger act of his own. Feeling guilty showing animals that other people had trained, David then retired Pat's lions, giving them a big yard to live in as exhibit animals. David explained his reluctance to show others' work. "People in a circus audience think that whatever they're seeing was trained by the presenter, but that's not always so. I felt like I was pulling the wool over someone's eyes because I didn't train the cats. I just get satisfaction knowing I trained them from scratch."

Daily between leopard performances, David trained a second big cat act, involving two tigers and one lioness. For one trick in this act, David trained the lioness, Tina, to sit up in front of him, and a tiger to jump over the two of them.

As he grew up, Tim also has been a part of the acts at the parks. Prior to the 1980s, Tim had presented snakes, and developed a liberty pony drill. As an adult he presented informative alligator lectures, and narrated David's cat shows. In the mid-1980s Tim backed up David's tiger and lion act. After presenting this act six summers, the brothers decided to work more closely together.

I had a chance to get to know Tim when he visited the Naples park for four days during spring semester break from Ohio State University. We began by talking about that time when he worked with David, and tigers, Bengal, and Prince, and Tina, the lioness. Tim explained that in the summer of 1988, David taught him to present the act. "I'd spent all my time on the outside of the cage, but when I first stepped in I had to relearn the whole routine."

3.11 David and Tina doing the shoulder stand.

Training is more complicated than it looks. "You'd think after watching an act for several years as a back-up I would have known what the trainer does, but I didn't, because I hadn't been watching the trainer. I was only watching the cats because that is where you should be looking," said Tim. He learned the routine by walking behind David, mimicking his movements in the ring. Within a week the brothers reversed roles for a few days; Tim cued the cats and David watched from behind. The progression continued: David stood in the back of the arena, then he was watching from outside the arena. This entire process took less than a month. Tim said, "That's great that I was able to do it so quickly, but if Dave hadn't put the proper training into the act it would have been a fiasco."

Tim excitedly spoke of the first time Bengal, the tiger, jumped over his head. "The pedestals and you are positioned so there's an even flow when the tiger jumps from a lower pedestal to a higher pedestal, over your head to the higher, then to lower pedestals on the other side, then to the ground and back to his place. When he's on the medium pedestal his eyes are about even with mine. Then Bengal comes and you see his feet, then he's over you. What a rush—that animal going over me and then going back to his seat.

"Dave had also trained the lioness, Tina, to stand in front of him and put her paws on his shoulders so he's face-to-face with a lion. There must be a lot of trust on the part of that animal. She's probably feeling kind of funky with her paws on a person's shoulders, exposing all her belly. When I presented that trick, a lot of times she'd go up and immediately come down—THUNK. Tina was more comfortable with her paws on David's shoulders and stayed in that position longer on him than me."

Although Tim thoroughly enjoyed working with chimps, ponies, and David's big cats, Tim shares David's reluctance to present animals trained by others. "It's like a person does an oil painting and another person puts a frame on it and talks about all the framing they did on it. The main work is the painting. The time David has put in seven days a week for more than ten years is what matters."

Although Tim did a fine job presenting the act, after a month, Prince refused to work for him. Unfortunately there was no way David could work with Tim or Prince to ensure Tim's safety. If an animal refuses to work, the Tetzlaffs do not try to coerce it.

David's act changes as his abilities grow and the American audiences' taste matures. For one early trick he had the animals jump through a hoop of fire. "That was when I was trying to be like everybody else. I eventually dropped it after I read a circus review that said some tricks are passé, like jumping through fire." David said with animation, "I thought: *They're right! It's a passé trick and doesn't belong.* Some good trainers still do it, arguing that jumping through fire is the epitome of the wild animal act.

But I don't want to see it and it's my act so you can like what I do or not like what I do. Jumping through a hoop of fire is not one of the cats' natural behaviors."

3.12 (Left to right) René Strickler, Jim Clubb, David Tetzlaff, and Louis Knie at the Circus Knie in Europe.

3.13 European trainer, Emil Smith, with leopard.

3.14 (Left to right) David in Europe with Marcel Peters, Dickie Chipperfield, Jr., and Jim Clubb.

3.15 David (third from left) with David Jamieson, editor of *King Pole* magazine, and trainers Jim Clubb, and Sacha Houck.

Audiences always smile and applaud the acts, but David notices if one little piece is imperfect. Although he is attuned to the big cats and feels confident handling them, he is less confident with people, sometimes appearing moody and unsure of himself. His perfectionism breeds success but also private discontent.

Paul Pifer said, "Dave has never been the extrovert that his father was. David is an animal person. If you give him the choice of spending his time with a bunch of people or a bunch of animals—he won't hesitate. I honestly believe if he had his druthers he'd train in a secluded spot, just him and the cats and would prefer not to have an audience."

3.16 Tim and David share the Cedar Point arena with big cats.

In recent years David has changed, improving his relationship to the audience. "I've cared about how I show the act. Before I was mainly concerned about training the tricks." Nancy elaborated, "David felt the animals were the stars and he was insignificant. Now he realizes that he is just as important as the animals."

David is always seeking new challenges. He enjoys creating mixed acts, putting together natural enemies or those species not found on the same continent, such as an act showing the behaviors of coexisting tigers, lions, and zebras. His father was known for these "harmony acts," as is David's trainer-friend, Jim Clubb.

David's International Status

Earlier, in 1984, an article in *Circus Report* magazine called David one of the top animal trainers in America. When David had been training cats for only four years his act consisted of seven leopards. Soon he surpassed this achievement by presenting seventeen leopards performing numerous behaviors—all in one act. Only two other trainers had worked with more leopards—Alfred Court in the 1940s with eighteen leopards, and Gunther Gebel-Williams, who before his retirement in 1990, used twenty-two leopards. David's reputation was growing.

Aside from following in his famous father's footsteps, and making his own name popular, David is a media celebrity. He's been on TV in Florida and throughout the Midwest, taking small animals to show and tell about—baby leopards, jaguars, alligators, lizards, snakes, a mona monkey, and anything small enough to take in a studio.

The media seeks stories behind David's success. In 1991, he was featured in *People* magazine. The following spring, FUJI TV flew a camera crew over from Japan to film a day in the life of David Tetzlaff.

3.17 Josip Marcan is dwarfed by a liger, a cross between a lion father and a tiger mother.

For several years, David has written articles on various topics for *King Pole* magazine. He presented a series of circus reports about his 1992 trip to England, Germany, and Switzerland. He said he gets a kick out of writing the articles. "I like to write, when I have the time. For that trip, I wrote five different reviews for *Circus Report*." He meticulously goes through his notes and examines the programs to see if he missed an act or a person he should write about.

David told me, "The finest compliment I ever got was when David Jamieson, editor of *King Pole* magazine saw my act in 1988 and compared it to Gunther Gebel-Williams, Dickie Chipperfield, Jr., and James

Clubb. He said my act was as good as they were. This was the highest praise because they are my idols, my heroes in the business."

David accidentally became sort of a goodwill ambassador when he helped Sarwat Begbudi, an animal trainer from Russia. Begbudi initially had planned to be in the states only a few weeks the summer of 1990 to buy four white tigers. At that time, Josip Marcan was one of only four trainers in the world who had some for sale. Begbudi met Marcan in Ohio where he was performing, to look over the tigers in person.

Jim Cole, Marcan's representative in the United States, told me about helping David and Marcan get his white tigers together for Begbudi. "David had an option to buy one of Marcan's white tigers, Natasha. However, the Russians wanted to buy all four. So David brought Natasha from Cedar Point to Cleveland, and I brought the other three from Florida. We presented them to Sarwat. Then we discovered the tigers had to be in quarantine thirty days before overseas shipment. David offered to quarantine them at Cedar Point. The tigers and Sarwat ended up staying most of that summer because of one bureaucratic foul up after another." The extended stay gave Sarwat and David the opportunity to become great friends.

3.18 David shares a special moment with Russian friends Olga and Sarwat Begbudi, and their white tigers at Cedar Point.

David has maintained friendships with most of his competitors. About twenty people in the United States train and present a variety of animals—too few trainers to have a conference. (The exception is elephant trainers and marine mammal trainers who have an annual conference.) The most big cat trainers David has been with at any one time is four. David especially enjoys spending time with, and the friendship of James Clubb and Josip Marcan. He says he's a sponge. "I soak up the knowledge. When you're the young trainer, you don't talk unless asked. Just having a meal with someone, or watching somebody practice or train, I always learn a little something.

"Jim Clubb and I went to Deerfield Beach a couple years ago and watched Josip. We were sitting there when Jim said, 'He's a true professional.' For Clubb to say that of somebody who's a competitor took a lot, because trainers very rarely compliment each other. We spend more time putting each other down than we do building each other up. Just sitting in Marcan's trailer with Clubb—two of the greatest trainers in the world—and they're both friends of mine. I just shut up and listened. It's kind of a neat feeling being the upstart hanging around these guys."

3.19 Trainer John Cox performing a shoulder stand with a white tiger.

On occasion, David will ask Clubb for advice. David had trained a few hind-leg walking cats before meeting Clubb, who later taught David a new method for it. "When I was training a leopard to do the hind-leg walk, I used the method I saw Clubb doing in England but was not quite right. I called Jim up and told him what I was doing and then the next Christmastime we were together and he helped me fix it. I usually prefer my methods for training everything but not for the hind-leg walk."

I asked David who were the other top professional trainers in the late 1980s when his leopard act was at its zenith? He told me they were Gunther Gebel-Williams and John Cox, both retired now. "Cox had fourteen tigers working as good as anything Gunther ever did. He worked in America and Japan for the Hawthorne Circus and was a very good trainer."

David told me his current competition is Ron Whitfield who has "the best cat act in America. Whitfield, a trainer at a big park in northern California, has fourteen tigers and lions. He's the best trainer, with the best act. Wade Burck at Ringling Brothers is very good. Wayne Franzen has his own circus and is good with lions and tigers. Lilli-Ana Christianson has a leopard act with eight leopards. Those are people that I know personally—it's hard to make judgments on others I don't know."

3.20 Ron Whitfield performing the Roman Ride with two seven-year-old Bengal tigers. (courtesy Darryl Bush, Marine World/Africa USA)

Friends and Competitors

"David's approach to animal training and care is in keeping with the way things are today. Years ago when the trainer went in the cage, it was the savage beasts versus the man. The man was the hero and anything he could do to the beasts was justified because they were trying to eat him alive," said Jim Cole. "Now the public doesn't buy that. The public is more conscientious about animals. Animals are beautiful creatures that deserve to be treated with dignity.

"I've heard David talk about some trainers, saying they teach the cats to run before they can walk. So David teaches to stay on your seat, sit up, come when you're called, go back to the pedestals. Then all the other tricks evolve from that, if the cat is capable of learning them."

Mike Cecere concurred, volunteering a similar assessment in our phone conversation. "David trains as it should be done. He does things at the proper pace so it's easy on the animals and he shapes their confidence so they make the most difficult tricks look easy."

Pat White said, "I have trained lions and tigers for seventeen years. When I worked at Jungle Larry's African Safari from 1974 to 1976, David was in his early teens and had not started his career with the animals. In about 1990 I saw David's leopard act.

It was absolutely fabulous. Much to my surprise and delight, his twelve leopards did absolutely everything Gunther's did. David is a very competent animal trainer.

"He's worked very hard to get where he is now. My only regret is that he hasn't had the nationwide exposure he deserves, because he has chosen to stay in the park. Even

3.21 Trainer Lilli-Ana Christianson waltzing with a leopard. (photo courtesy of Lilli-Ana)

3.22 Wayne Franzen with his mixed lion/tiger act.

though there are a lot of visitors in both parks he doesn't get that one-on-one exposure like if he was on a show moving around to different communities. Certainly the *People* magazine article was terrific, but people forget so quickly. He ought to have the fame that Gunther has, because he's certainly got the talent."

Roy Wells, who taught David to present the park's elephants said, "When I recently visited Jungle Larry's, somebody asked David where he got his start and he pointed me out in the audience. That was kind of fun. He's always been a real good humble kid and eager to learn whatever he can."

Another admirer of David is former zoo director, Frank Thompson, who became an animal supplier, buying animals from American zoos and shipping them to zoos overseas.

Thompson had this praise of David: "I saw

3.23 Wade Burck, astride a Bengal tiger.

him do a seven-cat simultaneous rollover—a truly spectacular stunt. The thing that stands out the most is that David is a gentle animal trainer. I wish that many years ago I had had the nerve or whatever it might have taken to do exactly what he's doing today. I envy him and I think the world of him. David is a big, lanky guy, as I was when I started out. Of course, this does not make for a very flashy-looking act, particularly with smaller animals, such as leopards. Leopards are so fast and think so quickly. It makes them very difficult to train. In spite of this, David produced a very fine leopard act. But his size alone tends to overwhelm the viewer in terms of comparison size with the leopards. To his credit, in spite of this he went ahead and produced some very fine performing cats."

Jungle Larry's Cedar Point Operations Manager Art Kozlik commented, "I was impressed when I first saw David work on the leopards. I'd seen all the big acts in my lifetime, starting when I accompanied my grandfather who was with the Hegenback-Wallace Circus. Because David's a perfectionist, he's achieved something very few leopard trainers have. I don't think anybody in the world I've ever seen on tape accomplished as much as David did with his twelve leopards."

David feels that any honors and achievements should be based on honest effort. "I want to be in the business for the right reasons." This is why he spends so much time with his animals, doing all the chores himself instead of hiring help, and staying up all night if an animal is giving birth. He cares about this extended family, not the glamour of performing on TV.

But the work is also demanding and dangerous. "People my age or younger see me in Cedar Point and say, 'Wow! How do you get in this business?' You can't. Forget it. It's hard to get into, hard to stay alive. Would these people feel the same in the hospital getting stitched? Or doing the hours of cleaning? All they see is someone kissing a tiger and getting applause for it. They also may see me out there raking the cage, and they think, 'Yuk. Look at that job.' They don't realize that's the same guy who was in the ring. You've got to take both jobs."

David remembers his father's advice: Don't get yourself in a situation where you need someone else to get you out. "If you're doing that, you don't belong in there. Always know you're going to have to get yourself out of that situation first. Then if you can't someone will have to help, but don't subject someone else's safety to your stupidity," said David.

Because Ringling is well known for its safety, animal welfare, and top shows, David has always admired Ringling's trainers. But he pointed out that those trainers not only had to do their work; each had to have a unique image, often developed by Ringling.

"Gunther always got so much media attention. I think to a lot of people Gebel-Williams [on the Red Show] was the only trainer in the world. Ringling Brothers always pushed him in the media. Wade Burck now is on another Ringling tour, but from 1984 to 1988 he was Gunther's competitor on Ringling's Blue Show. Ringling markets a trainer the way they think he would appeal to the public. So for Gunther, they brought over this blond, sequined, tireless Aryan superstar who worked twenty-four hours a day—Gunther's image. But for Wade they created more of a caring environmentalist trainer. I guess Wade is kind of like that. I've become that way on my own, without Ringling Brothers or any company dictating I have to act that way."

David's dream used to be to work for Ringling Brothers Circus or to train animals at Jungle Larry's and to send acts to other parts of the country. David admits he no longer cares about that. "For awhile I had stars in my eyes, but the bottom line is you're in the ring with the animals. If you're good, you're good, no matter where you are. It took me a long time to realize this."

David's biggest regret is that his father is not here to see his accomplishments. "I took this life-style for granted growing up. Looking back there was nothing like it, having a famous father. My dad never had a big ego. And that's what helps me keep perspective."

4

Building a
Relationship

You can't just click the animals on on Monday and off on Friday. They need feeding, care, and attention all the time. Everything I have I owe them. Without them, I'm nothing. I'm not a trainer without these guys. —David Tetzlaff

A S WE ENTERED the restricted area that houses and shelters a dozen tigers, I asked David how much time he spends working. He replied that he works fourteen-hour days, with half a day off a week. "Most of the time I'm in rubber boots. The show is actually a small part of what goes on here." It's his job to care for these animals. It is also his nature. Hosing down a 5000-square-foot tiger's cage floor (while the tigers are two cages down) David said, "I like all aspects of this. To me it's almost equal whether I'm cutting up the cats' meat, feeding them, washing down their cages, training, or doing the show. I think of them as "people" and I think I'm closer to my animals than a lot of trainers are. I do a lot of close contact and I can put my hands on all the cats. I think my being in with them so much adds up to that total cooperation between the cats and myself."

Many other trainers in other shows and circuses do only the arena work and hire grooms to feed the animals and clean their cages. Sometimes when laboring so much, David thinks "Jeez, why do I do all this myself?" But the alternative can cause problems, he explained. "You have grooms and others feeding and poking at the cats. If someone has been poking at them, they can go in the arena ticked off and you are the one to face it." Yet while performing, David sometimes tells his back-up, "Nudge him; he's not paying attention," to keep the cat alert. David thinks that his closeness to his cats pays off in the long run. It's because he spends so much time with the animals that he gets along so well with them.

4.1 A lesson in international cooperation—Kiki, an African elephant, allows Amber, an Indian leopard to ride on her back.

During a typical day, from 7:00 to 9:00 A.M., David cleans the cats' cages. Then for an hour he cuts meat for that day's feeding. At 10:40 David and an assistant take the tigers to the arena for his 11:00 show, after which they return the cats to their cages. Shortly after noon David feeds the leopards, then exercises them in the ring while eating his own lunch. This takes until nearly 2:00, when he may have a tiger training session until 2:30. After a short break, David conducts his afternoon tiger show at 3:00. He feeds the tigers around 4:00 and leaves the park between 5:30 and 6:30. Although Jungle Larry's has a night watchman, David returns to the park to recheck the animals' health, security and cage locks for about half an hour, sometime between 8:00 and 10:00 P.M.

Between these routine daily activities, David manages to coordinate staff and answer their questions. Every Wednesday all of the staff members involved with animals attend a safety meeting. David also meets with Nancy Jane as needed.

He also reads and replies to correspondence and plans show changes as needed or inspired. He orders meat once a month for the cats and annually vaccinates all of the big cats. Somehow David finds time to keep up with trends by reading trade journals, visiting other parks and zoos and talking to other trainers. But despite all these activities, David always puts the animals first.

One day I came to the meat house to interview David while he worked. Approaching the small building, I heard Bruce Springsteen blasting away. David looked up and said, "Sorry," as he turned the radio off. "I'm used to cutting meat with loud music on."

While sharpening knives, he told me what the big cats eat: beef, chicken, and a commercial product called carnivore diet. A complete meal on its own, carnivore diet looks like ground beef. The entire cow is ground—something David calls "Elsie in a Cuisinart."

Before the development of special carnivore and feline diets, Jungle Larry's bought meat directly from the slaughterhouse. Larry once remarked, "There's no food given to those animals that you, yourself, couldn't eat." Today Jungle Larry's provides special diets to the cats. Inspectors mark the meat prepared for exotic cats at zoos with black charcoal to indicate that it is not to be used for human consumption, although nothing is wrong with it. Still, David is careful to check the condition of the meat, disposing of any doubtful pieces. The cats especially enjoy the cold meat in the summer as the ice crystals melt in their hot mouths. David's clean hands cut chicken and beef parts and apportion it with a carnivore diet, weighing it and scooping in powdered vitamins, then putting it into individual serving packages for easy distribution.

The various cat species eat different amounts of food: tigers consume at least ten pounds per day; lions, sixteen or seventeen pounds; male leopards, about six; and female leopards, about three pounds. One day a week when they are not working, the cats have only a bone. "Bone days" give their stomachs a rest and simulates eating in the wild where the big cats would not catch food every day. The weather has a lot to do with the cats' food consumption. When the days are hot, they eat less; when the nights are cool, they need more. Altogether the Tetzlaffs have about four dozen big cats who consume 350 to 425 pounds of meat per day. The annual cost to feed just the cats in this zoo is about $44,000.

David and an assistant distribute the food to the leopards around noon. On a typical day, David wears shorts, a light shirt, and gym shoes. As I accompanied him, a leopard by his foot playfully tried to bite it. David gently moved the leopard away with his foot and said, "Come on, Sabrina, stop that."

After the big cats have had lunch, they get exercise in the arena—an hour or so for a couple or three tigers, then it's time to switch to leopards. He sits on a stool and eats his lunch while the cats run or walk around. The cats don't beg for food while David lunches. On the contrary, the leopards rub against his legs or roll over on their backs to be petted while he eats.

Keeping Big Cats Healthy

When asked if he ever needs to bathe a cat David said, "No. I spray them down on real hot days. Mix water with fly spray to cool them and discourage flies."

What about fleas? David seemed surprised at my question. He said Jungle Larry's has never had a cat with fleas, except once when David purchased two neglected tigers and a lion who were skinny and had their hair falling off. "I just felt sorry for them, so I bought them. Got them looking nice and then sold them. That was the first time I saw fleas on wild animals." David's eyes narrowed as he said, "NONE of our animals have fleas. That's why I was freaked out to see fleas on those animals. Defleaing tiger or lion cubs is not a fun thing to do."

When I met him at his clean, spacious Naples office, Dr. Jeffrey Noble, the veterinarian for Jungle Larry's, said diseases have not been a problem at the park. The cats are vaccinated (once a year; more often when first born) for feline distemper and respiratory ailments.

They've never experienced feline leukemia, heartworms, or feline infectious peritonitis (FIP—a virus). "Jungle Larry's animals are a very healthy group of animals—the whole group," the vet remarked.

Dr. Noble said that because David can go right up to the animals without their being leery of him, he is able to vaccinate the cats himself. David sometimes used to put the cats in the safety cages and have the vet do it from the outside, but "they freak out; they know something's going on."

Now David always does it personally. He said, "I go in there with a couple of syringes in my pocket and nonchalantly walk up. It's over with quickly; I think they don't feel it. It takes practice though."

When an animal needs oral medication, sometimes the Tetzlaffs have to be sneaky to be successful. The animals easily pick up the scent of medicine. Nancy told me, "Ideally we take a big chunk of beef and stick the pill in a pocket of the meat. The animals are good about finding it, even the cubs eating the ground carnivore diet. Many times after the animal is finished eating there's that pill left in the dish. So we make a meatball. Stick the pill in and throw the food right down the mouth. It's easier with a cub; you can stick it way back in the mouth so they have no choice. The bigger cats keep getting little balls until they take it."

Charly Baumann, the animal trainer of the 1940s and 1950s, fed his animals one live animal, usually a chicken, per month. When his cats were sick, he fed them a live chicken four days in a row because of the medicinal properties in whole, live animals (something tigers would be catching in the wild) and to improve their morale. The extra dose of live food usually helped the cats get well faster. Years later Larry fed the big cats a fresh-killed rabbit weekly. Larry felt that internal organs were good for the cat, and the hair served as a natural de-wormer (like a brush going through intestines). David and Nancy no longer feed fresh-killed prey to their big cats because it is now unnecessary to their diet and health.

When asked about care of sick cats, David said, "Every animal trainer has stayed up all night with a sick animal. If they've had an operation, we stay with them until they come out of it. You'd hate for something to happen and not be there. Last year a leopard, Kaley, had one cub; she was fine at first but sick the next day. We had to rush her to the vet's for an emergency cesarean. Dr. Noble pulled out another cub, a dead one. Kaley would have died from infection if the cub hadn't been removed. I stayed until she came around."

Handling Cats

Because trainers make their relationship with the big cats seem so comfortable, observers may think that the big cats can be handled by absolutely anyone. That's an illusion. The trainer-cat relationship has been developed through hard work over a long period of time, as David explained.

4.2 Friend, Eileen Hofmaster (left) and park employee, Becky Speer share a moment with Maya, the jaguar cub.

Trainers often speak of "breaking" an animal as meaning training it. David inhaled deeply and said, "It's a rough-sounding word but it's what we all say. You start off breaking a bronco—breaking a horse's spirit. I'm not trying to do that. The word actually doesn't apply. I'm trying to train them, but I never want them to forget that they're a tiger. I never want to demean this animal to thinking he's something less than what he is, because to me I could not have a true leopard or tiger show anymore."

Despite David's continual presence, many months' contact are required before he can pet an unfamiliar cat. Getting close to a big cat is easier if it is young, which is often possible at Jungle Larry's because many animals are raised from birth. Becky Speer, a longtime park employee, is one of the few who has hand-raised a cub for David. She and another employee who has also raised a cub agreed: "We can raise the cubs and they're attached to us somewhat, but as soon as Dave shows up they immediately love him."

Becky continued, "I don't know what it is about him. When David returns from Cedar Point to the animals at Naples that haven't seen him for months, they immediately respond to him."

Many of the big cats that came to Jungle Larry's in the late 1960s (before the passage of the Endangered Species Act) were hand-raised, and have in turn given birth at the park. Other cubs were acquired from people in the business. Leopard cubs cost $800 to $1,500, lions and tigers $500 to $5,000. The higher prices are for tigers with white genes, indicated by the animal or one of its ancestors being born in a litter that also contained a white tiger.

Favorite Cats

During a walk one day to the meat house, David admitted to having a fondness for special cats. We walked along the path past an immense fig tree, a traveler's palm, and shell ginger near the alligators while David reminisced about some of his cats, most of whom he raised. "Probably my favorite cat was Pepé, a jaguar cub I had when I was four or five years old." When David was ten years old he had a lion cub named Charley, who used to sleep on his bed with him. Charley was one of sixteen cubs the Tetzlaffs had at one time, before selling some of them to another park and some to a circus act.

David continued, "That's looking way back. Now my favorites are these guys [pointing to his tigers]. All are doing their best for me in their own way. Some like me more than others." He also feels more comfortable with some than others. "I can get away with more with leopards than with tigers, due to sheer size. Because the leopards trust me, and because they're ninety to one hundred thirty pounds, tops, I can pick most of them up. If an animal doesn't want to be handled like that, of course I don't pick them up. With the new tiger I can get away with some stuff, too; Nirvana is slow—the way she thinks and moves—so I can physically move her around and stand closer to her."

But he stresses caution. "You shouldn't trust any of them. Last Christmas Eve I was teaching Nirvana the shoulder stand when her claw caught and split my ear, requiring nine stitches. Can't blame the animal. She just got careless. The trainer always pays the price. I never drew blood on an animal in my life. I'm the one who gets stitches."

4.3 David walking a young tiger on leash to the delight of the park visitors.

The young tigers are walked individually on a leash. I walked about eight feet behind David one day as he clomped alongside ten-month-old Shikar, who playfully kept biting David's boot. David stopped him: "Quit! Enough!" Shikar was born in the Clyde Beatty Circus but spent his first few months growing up in a zoo. David had acquired him just three months earlier. David continued, "After closing the other day, I leashed Shikar and let him walk in the office. Just fun for me. And fun for him and for the office people."

As we walked, between the "stop-it" exclamations to Shikar, David became nostalgic. Prince, the oldest tiger in the act, has been with David since cubhood. For his first year of life, Prince slept in the Tetzlaff house on David's queensize bed with him.

"Even when Prince got big, I used to take him on a leash and let him swim in the pond. But the more animals you get the less time you have for individuals, which is unfortunate."

When I asked about the difficulty of dealing with animals that were not hand-raised, David responded, "It's a matter of the time you put in with the animal. I got one black leopard when he was seven years old. He had never seen me before and tried to chase me out of the cage. The animal gradually became affectionate and was eventually in my lap, but it took seven months. In modern training, the animal must respect the trainer and enjoy performing as requested." The respect and closeness are mutual. When David walks by their cages, the animals again show affection by chuffling and rubbing against the cage.

Said David, "If I were an animal I'd probably be a cat. I know really good cat trainers definitely have an aura around them and you can see it's there and the cats feed off that.

"I don't like dogs in general, because dogs like everybody. A friend of mine has a dog and it's nice. I'm not going to knock it, but I just like cats. Cats are picky."

Sometimes the relationship with a big cat begins by choosing a personalized name for the animal. Nancy said, "When you look at a big cat you think of royalty; Prince and Princess were our first pair of lions. It seemed natural. Later, Prince and Bengal were two of the first names chosen for tigers. One consideration is the command of a name: 'PRINCE!' You don't usually want more than two syllables in a name for the vocal."

One might think that two very similar names could cause confusion. With a Prince and a Princess in same arena, could a trainer call one and have the other respond by mistake? Nancy said this wasn't a problem, because the trainer looks at the cat being addressed.

David takes time naming his cats. Sometimes he thinks of a name and saves it for the right animal. He uses traditional big cat and human names. Every trainer seems to use certain popular names. "Prince and Bengal—those are my concession to tradition. There have been other leopards besides mine with the name Java; Alfred Court had a cat by that name and Jim Clubb has one. I named my lion Tina, because Gunther's [Gebel-Williams] stepdaughter is named Tina. Silly ways like that. I have almost all of the animals for awhile before naming them." Names sometimes come to him after he gets to know a particular animal. He is sometimes inspired by books. For example, "A tiger I had, Sackett, I named after a family Louis L'Amour writes about. They originally came from England and settled in the Carolinas and pushed westward and they're tough, gritty people—that's kind of the way Sackett was. So that was a good name."

David added, "I've gotten superstitious in the last couple years. I changed Nirvana's name when she was still little, because her original name, Tora, was a bad luck name. Marcan previously had a cat named Tora that got hold of three people. Then he named Nirvana, 'Tora.' I didn't want that. Actually I shouldn't have called Bengal 'Bengal' either; that's bad luck. Alfred Court had a 'Bengal' that killed two people. But it's too late to change the name he's had for years.

"Sometimes you have a name you know you want to use. Shikar means tiger hunt. The Indian word is like the Asian version of safari. Kind of one of those twisted-irony names. I never heard of a tiger named Shikar either, so I thought it was a good name."

Injuries, Risks, and a Close Call

Perhaps the primary consideration for a trainer is how to stay alive. Long periods of safe contact with big cats can lead to a false sense of security, and Jim Cole, who knows many of the top trainers, such as James Clubb, Michael Cecere, Pat White, and David, provided an example: "David told me last year a tiger grabbed him. I said 'Well, David, what do you expect? You get used to the cats being so good, then when one nails you it reminds you these are tigers you're working with.' That's the thing about the new approach [the loving style of animal training]. There's so much gentleness and you're not agitating the cats so that when they do something you say 'Hey, wait a minute. These *are* tigers. They're not house cats.' The public gets the wrong impression: 'Look how tame they are. He's out there petting them and they're not snarling at him or anything; they must be tame.' But they're not."

Art Kozlik related a dangerous incident that occurred when David was twenty. "This happened during a training session in Florida. David's black leopard, Missy, wasn't responding correctly to the shoulder carry. She was stubborn, so he decided he'd get another leopard to carry. He picked the biggest leopard he had. When he went in to practice, he forgot he had a cashmere sweater on. You shouldn't wear anything an animal can get his claws into. We cleared the arena, and I brought this leopard in, a male named Taj. I was working as back-up outside the door. David put him on two pedestals, gave him a piece of meat, and went underneath to pick him up. But Taj did not want to go up on the shoulders and let David know it. So David dumped him, gave him another piece of meat. I warned him, 'David, don't try it. He doesn't want to go up.' David had had the animals since they were cubs, but this was an older animal. Yet it's one he used to lie down with in the act. So he went back in there again and this time Taj got his claws into that soft material and didn't like the feel of it or something. He didn't want to be lifted up. He nailed David's neck with his teeth, then dug his claws and feet into David's side.

"Taj got David down on the floor and he couldn't move. The cat had an awful grip on his arm and shoulder. I went into the arena with a broomstick handle we used and I couldn't get it in the animal's mouth. I whacked him four or five times across the head. David's yelling at me, 'In the mouth! In the mouth!' I said, 'David, I can't get it in his mouth the way he's got you.' I swung a good hard one and missed the leopard and hit David in the head. It took seven stitches to close up his head. It wasn't bad enough the leopard was giving him a terrible time, but I clobbered him myself and did more damage to his head. I won't tell you what David yelled at me. Then Taj moved. I got the stick down his throat and got him off David and the minute I got Taj away from David, David was up on his feet and I backed out of the arena and he took over putting the cat away, even though he was bleeding and hurting.

"When he's on his feet, the trainer is in control and the back-up no longer belongs in the ring. The rule of thumb when you're working back-up as a trainer: You *never* go into the arena to help a trainer unless he's down on the ground and he cannot handle himself any longer; that's the only time. Otherwise, he can handle the animal far better than you can. Larry Tetzlaff had always impressed me with that and so did David.

"Later we laughed about the incident. People used to come in to lectures and ask David, 'Ever get hurt? What was the worst experience you ever had?' David told them, a whole big crowd,

'Worst experience? I had my head split open and it took seven stitches to close it up—and that was from my back-up!' "

Tim remembered that "David's patched himself up many times. A couple of summers ago a big tiger ripped through his back and I cleaned him up before he went to the hospital." He grinned, "We've cleaned each other up—a nice way for brothers to draw closer to each other, 'So this is what your muscles look like,' " Tim kidded David.

Tim used to back up David. "I've never had to go in with David when he's been in trouble, but there were some tight moments. One time he was doing the leopard blanket when all the leopards were on top of him. I saw one of the leopards open her mouth right at head level and I had enough time—one or two seconds—to say something. But the animal was not doing it maliciously. And I didn't want to have Dave turn his head because that would have increased the danger. So I just watched and she clipped through his eyebrow—you can see a white streak through his eyebrow where her tooth went. I'm not enough of a leopard psychologist to know what she was thinking then, but she didn't seem to be playing, and yet it wasn't 'I'm mad at you and I'm going to get you.' I mean here she is in a totally loving way on top of him. If she had been irritated, the first thing she would have done is get off him."

David added, "Getting hurt hurts. When your cat gets one claw in you it hurts. If he gets you by the neck, you're done: one bite and one shake and you're history. I guess that'd be better than suffering."

I asked David about the riskiest thing he's done. "I've done some things I should have been killed for. One time when I was twenty-one, a lion named Chubby came after me in the yard. Male lions can develop homosexual tendencies toward each other. When they do, they get possessive like they would over a female. When they do that, they just want you out of the way. I had worked these three lions in the show. One night the cats didn't want to go in the house [their cages]. They got possessive over each other. I used to work Chubby for the show, so I thought I could go in there and get him in the house. He charged me across the yard and knocked me down and clawed my leg. I knew the lions were hormonally stirred up, but when you're young you think you're invincible. Then you find out you bleed like everybody else."

David mentioned an old scar on his back that resulted from a scratch during a performance. "That's where I got fifteen stitches to close a scratch from a tiger. The audience knew I was hurt and I got a standing ovation at the end. Even though I was hurt, it was such a high—the people appreciating my finishing the act for them. After the *People* magazine article came out, many people asked me 'Which is the one that ate you up?' I don't ever tell which one it was. Everybody would look at that cat differently. Getting hurt is a great learning experience," David said with a smile. But he's also embarrassed about his injuries because he says they're caused by human error.

Kozlik agrees: "Most of the time, if the trainer gets hurt it's because he made a mistake himself. It's never the cat's fault. You did something wrong."

The trainer takes most of the risk. It's rare at Jungle Larry's when an animal is injured. I asked if the big cats ever have a problem similar to house cats eating string or thread that slices through their intestines. David said they take precautions so that doesn't happen. Yet when Bengal was a year or so old he ate a corner of a tarp that had blown into his cage. It had been put up to block wind on a cold night. "For three weeks we didn't know if we'd have to cut him open. Pretty scary. Finally it all worked out of his intestines."

Paul Pifer talked about when he and David worked at Jungle Larry's as teens. "We didn't have very many sick or injured animals. As far as sick animals go, I wasn't there when it occurred, but I remember David was doing a practice session in the arena when one of his black cats was spooked by an onlooker's loud prank and bounced off the side of the performance arena. The cat jumped from too great a height and landed on his side getting badly injured. The cat was examined by their Ohio vet, Dr. Dean Kraus. It had internal injuries and died. David was just devastated. To him they're people. They're not animals, they're people. You'd think a parent had died or something."

Fear and Respect

Larry had strong feelings about the right way to train animals—guidelines his family follows today. Nancy Jane recalled his words: "Some trainers alter their animals by declawing and defanging; we call these people 'vegetable trainers.' If you can't train animals the way they're made, you have no business being a trainer. All our cats have their claws and teeth."

By allowing the cats to keep their claws and teeth, the family has a healthy respect for the potential for danger. Tim described his feelings after leaving the arena where he had just been with David and some leopards: "I'm floating on air because I'm safe out here. If I trip right now, I'm not going to die. If I had tripped in there, I could have died."

Some trainers say they're always scared, others say it's all bluff anyway. About his fear, David looked at me and said, "I feel I've inherited my dad's guts. I've been scared maybe four times out of thousands of shows, but I usually didn't let it show. So far it hasn't been enough for me to stop this and go work at a grocery store. When I am scared, I don't really fear for my own sake: You're always afraid of the animals messing up or fighting with each other."

4.4 Jim Cole and David with a golden tabby tiger.

Paul agreed with David's view of himself. "I can remember the time he was chewed pretty badly while doing the shoulder carry. It's the old 'get-back-on-the-horse' thing. It's going to make you a little nervous the next time you do that when you remember the pain you went through the last time. But as far as sweating, pacing, rubbing his hands together and so on, I don't ever remember him looking jittery."

On the other hand, David doesn't boast. "That's not why I'm in it. Every trainer has a cat that'll roar at him and some trainers still try to play up on that. I just don't see the point in it. I'm not out here trying to be macho man.

"Some trainers get hurt because they didn't carefully choose the animals they trained and tended to train every animal they could acquire. I know two trainers in Europe, father and son; neither has a scar, and the father is eighty-four years old. They're just careful. No matter what your situation, you need to learn to focus. That's the whole key to staying alive. You can buy the farm every day you go in there."

Even if a trainer works with a tiger or leopard from an early age, the dangers are considerable. The independence of tigers makes it hard for them to take orders. In groups, sometimes they fight and injure themselves and trainers can get hurt by interceding.

"In some ways leopards are more dangerous—they're smaller and faster, and they fight for the pleasure of it. However, in fourteen years of training and performing, David has found these skirmishes infrequent. "When introducing new animals to the act you can expect some conflicts. If you're going to have an act you always need to introduce new animals. Sometimes they accept each other right away, sometimes they don't. In training, Centaine, an adult trained tiger has been lying down next to the babies [two younger tigers in training] for two months and she's never tried to grab one once. But Delhi's just sneaky." Delhi is an another adult trained tiger who sometimes tries to bite the younger cats. David explained how to minimize risk. "You can't relax in the cage. You must be ready to handle any lightning change in an animal. Leopards are especially dangerous. I've had leopards go for me four times in the last nine years. If a leopard wants to get you, he can attack from anywhere. Leopards can make a ninety-degree turn in the air."

Tim also spoke about the respect for leopards and tigers that came from living and working with the animals. He said, "One of David's leopards, Benjamin, used to take a real liking to me. He'd come over and brush against the fence when I came by. One morning my brother invited me in; that was the first time I ever felt a full-grown leopard's back. It's like a table, a solid sheet of muscle, it's so strong. You get an immediate respect for the power that's there, all tightened up in those vertebrae. The leopard thought that was okay for a little bit, but then he looked around, went behind a pedestal and looked up at me and Dave calmly said, 'I think you'd better get out, and I got out. Those cats have the ultimate respect for Dave."

Tim said that fear and respect go together. "If you're not a little bit afraid, part of your brain has been sucked out. I'm very aware of what horrible things man-eaters can do and what big cats have done to trainers. So you have a very strong respect for the animal you're working with. If you're not somewhat afraid to go in the cage every day, you don't belong there—you'll soon be carried out of the cage. But there are thrills in the animal cage I've never gotten from anything else—a five-hundred-pound animal fully capable of killing me and there's no law that said he can't. But he's getting along perfectly well with me and I'm even asking him to do some stuff and he's doing it and it's as if the animal thinks 'Great, now I'm going back to my seat. See you for the next behavior.' It's an amazing rapport."

David's words and actions concerning his cats show the sort of devotion found in lifelong human friendships. He and his mother believe that the animals share his feelings and that close relationships develop between any caring trainer and his cats.

Nancy said, "The cats seem to be tuned in to your thinking; they take verbal cues. David trains the cats to come to him. You cannot force a cat to come to you. It's not out of fear; it's because  the animal wants to. That suggests a bond, respect. Love and respect have a lot to do with each other. The fact that they want to be near you and are comfortable with you shows their warm feelings."

5.

Training Big Cats

Training is developing an animal's natural tendencies on cue. You can't force them. A lot of times you try to get an animal to do something and you see their heart and soul is not in it physically, emotionally, mentally—so forget it. Try it with another cat and that cat may zip right into it. —David Tetzlaff

WHEN DAVID first acquires a young tiger or leopard, he simply cares for it and earns its trust. Like most other trainers, he usually waits until the cub is about eleven months old before attempting to train it. The initial training can be as quick as five or six months or as long as a year and a half.

Although David prefers to begin with very young cubs, cats up to a year old that he acquires from others seem largely unaffected by their previous environments and therefore humanely trainable. But he refuses to disrupt the lives of older cats. All of his cats were born in captivity and hand raised by humans. "I don't train wild cats; that's like jailing. My cats' grandparents might have been in Bangladesh. That kind of thinking may seem stupid, but I have a lot of feelings for the animal's point of view."

Training, Presenting, and Handling

The dangers of training are lessened by the right approach. Clyde Beatty said that you can't trust the animal, but the animal must have absolute trust in the trainer. David adds that to the cat, the trainer is a parent figure. When David hand raises a cub, it sees him as its father. The dependence fosters trust. The close relationships also encourage mutual respect.

Some behaviors are more natural for cats to do so they are easier to train. These include sitting on command, lying down, and jumping through a hoop.

Other tricks are more difficult such as walking on hind legs, being draped over the trainer's shoulders (leopards, not tigers) and rolling over as a group. Once the animals know the tricks, the trainer still must assemble the individual tricks into a complete act.

5.1 David practicing the tiger act.

Usually, the audience assumes that the act they see was trained by the person in the ring. Often this is not true. Three distinct occupations may be involved: handler, presenter, and trainer. A handler helps to feed and transport the animals and provides basic care. The presenter guides the animals through their act. These animals may have been trained by someone else; the trainer takes green (untrained) animals and teaches them tricks.

David elaborated, "Some presenters work an act so long that they start to believe they've trained it. But the difference between training and presenting is like the difference between performing music you have written and just playing someone else's composition in public.

"If you can put a leash on a tiger and walk him, you're a handler. If you can take that tiger into the ring, teach him to sit up, walk backward on his hind legs, and jump through a hoop, then you're a trainer. In between you have people who can present trained animals. That also takes know-how, guts, and determination, but to do what I and my closest peers do—put a whole act together—that makes a trainer."

The distinctions among the three jobs seem sharper overseas. David explained, "When I was in Europe, I saw the trainer supervising everything, doing clean work, wearing a pressed polo shirt. The groom does the feeding and cleaning. It's getting that way in America—two different jobs. The trainer has a nice clear mind and is rested for the show. But I like doing both jobs. There may come a day when I can't do it because—and that's my greatest regret right now—I don't have enough time to devote to training. If I had all the time in the world to train I could be a lot better than I am." Although David is one of the best trainers, he's also a perfectionist.

Elements of Training

A number of elements must come together to make a good act: The teachable animals must know their tricks; the trainer must cue the animals and constantly watch them for any problem; the music must go well with the act. And the animals must be able to work with each other and do this in the presence of many people and unpredictable background noise.

David's former back-up, Jeff Bolling, remarked to me, "If you're consistent in training, the animal will give one hundred percent too. Usually any trainer can do whatever is necessary to straighten out an animal if he's uncooperative on a given day. But you can't make them perform. You have to make it fun for the animal and get them to trust people."

This trust includes getting accustomed to the sights and noises the animals will routinely hear when in the arena. David trains the animals to work with taped rock and roll music in the background and has staff sit very close, make noise and get up and leave during the act. As David explained, no matter how many times you announce before the act to please remain seated and quiet, one percent of the people will not. By training with the disturbances, the animals became accustomed to having people sit only seven feet away from them while they work. Unlike Jungle

Larry's, at most other shows in America people sit about thirty feet from the animals. Like his father did, David enthusiastically encourages people to get the full sights, sounds, and smells of the animals, and sitting closer helps them to do this.

David continued, "Some animals trained without lights and crowds can get stagefright. I train in front of people, which is an important advantage. Tigers don't mind people so much, but leopards, the minute they see someone, they're off their seat. Playing a radio while training helps too. My cats have to contend with a roller coaster in Ohio. Tigers get used to sleeping under the roller coaster. A circus cat might see all kinds of stuff but take him to a roller coaster and it might turn him inside out. Take my cats to a circus and they might freak out at spotlights and clowns. It's just whatever they get used to."

The training situation resembles that of students and teacher in a classroom: The animals' personalities, trainer's attitudes, and the atmosphere all have to come together for the best results. David said, "A mouthy kid in a teacher's class isn't useless; he may just be vocal about what the class is told to do. Just because a cat barks at me one time, I'm not going to be scared and not work with it. But if an animal is uncooperative—if it doesn't want to do some behavior—forget it. You can only reinforce what it likes doing." He told me, "I had one black leopard do a trick— jumping over a high rope and another leopard's head. [In the trick, the leopards walk on two tightly-strung parallel ropes. One leopard sits on them, while the other comes from behind and jumps over the sitting leopard.] She worked it nicely two years without a hitch. Then one day she wouldn't do it, so that was the end of it. You can't force them to do something they don't want to do. Critics come in and say an animal can be pushed to do anything. If that was possible, everyone would have an amazing act."

Leopards are particularly clever, always thinking of ways to outsmart the trainer. David had trained a leopard to jump, leap-frog-style first over another leopard and then a panther jumped over a leopard, all while walking on the parallel ropes. "One was taught to stand and the other to jump clear over a rope. Then the first leopard I trained to do it got lazy." Resignedly David said, "Sweet Pea still wanted to do the trick but as she was going over Benjamin, she would bite him in the hamstring. That would make him sit and she then wouldn't have to jump as high. He was supposed to be standing. They'd both walk in the same direction, so she'd be behind him and just reach down and bite him in his back leg and he'd sit and she'd jump over him. The things they think up! So when the leopard was biting the other I stopped that. Jet did it well though. She never cheated, but one day she just decided not to do it and that was the end of it."

5.2 Leopards get to look down on their trainer as they walk the double tightrope.

A trainer must have the temperament and ability not only to avoid injury, but also to teach and lead the cats. He or she must be disciplined and alert, even if tired, moody, or sick. Because his life may depend on it, a trainer is also very aware of details. I noticed David's concentration while he was sitting on a stool in the arena, eating a sandwich while four leopards were exercising loose around him. I, of course, sat outside the arena bars, taping our conversation. As we talked, he stopped to yell at the cats once in a while, and he almost always came back to the exact place in the sentence where he'd left off. The same was true for lengthy business interruptions.

While these characteristics may be part of a trainer's basic personality, success also requires the development of certain attitudes.

A Successful Attitude

David said, "The show is necessary, because it's what people come for. But some of my favorite time in the ring is training. I just love to see young animals progress and learn."

David began a session one afternoon with a leather pouch attached to his belt to carry chunks of meat for rewarding desired behavior. From just outside the arena, I asked him why the seven tigers, who are patiently waiting on their seats, don't simply attack him for the meat. He responded, "They would if I let them. This new one I'm working with, Shikar, sometimes comes and noses up to the meat. I smack him on the nose with my hand. The reason some people get in trouble is they let things go too far in an early stage. My contention has always been that if there's a problem, nip it in the bud. I've seen a cat take a broom away from somebody and they let him have the broom—didn't want to take it back from the cat. Wrong! Nobody does that to me. I'll get hurt getting that broom back, but I'm taking it back, because 'it's not yours; you don't start that garbage with me.' That's just my attitude. It sounds like I'm dominating that animal, but I'm not. I'm just teaching him some respect. If they start that kind of business pretty soon they've got your leg and will get possessive over it!

"Earning the cats' respect starts when they're small. I walk them around on the leash and if somebody starts to jump up and bite he gets smacked down. That's not going to stop the adult tiger from jumping on you, but hopefully you won't make that tiger get to that point. If you do, then it is your fault. Everything that goes on is basically your fault because you figure this animal doesn't know anything when you got it and everything he learns is from you or the environment that you put him in."

Although David is firm with cats, he also gives them freedom. He amplified, "Some people put a lunge [collar with a lead] on leopards because they come at you so fast. I have never felt I had to control leopards this way. In Europe they may use a lunge, but not a leash. Of the few leopard acts in America, most work on a leash, not just loose in the cage [like David does]. That's the American people's idea of a leopard act really. In Europe they would never do that."

Freedom and Responsibility

Allowing the cats freedom is related to an understanding of and respect for their psyches. For example, all cats fear open spaces and unfamiliar territory. Because an arena is a naturally vulnerable environment, especially for a new cat, compassion and sensitivity are important. The arena is connected to two holding pens, each by a chain-link chute. Until the animals are used to the ring, trainers leave a chute open so the animals can escape. "You never want to drive the animals in the ring and force them to stay there. They can leave if they want. You don't want them to feel trapped in the ring." David's approach is a subtle balance between constraint and freedom, discipline and care.

He described the importance of empathy and good sense. "Some people can see the world through the tigers' eyes, some only through human eyes—'I'm going to make this cat do this because it's what I want.' But if an animal is uncomfortable with something I'll drop it." Instead of forcing unnatural behavior, like having a tiger stand on a huge ball to make it roll slowly, David encourages natural tendencies: "In raising cubs, you observe them and see different traits. For example, when two cubs greet each other I might notice that one likes to go up on her hind legs, suggesting potential for hind-leg walking. Other cubs bounce all around from pedestal to pedestal during their acquaintance period, indicating an eagerness to jump."

David said that the trainer must control his emotions. "If you're in a bad mood, you may as well not even go in to train. You might mess up the session by being short-tempered, or getting fed up. I stop rather than force it. The cats have the same option. If the cats aren't up for it, forget it. Otherwise you can have problems. So much of the training is mental rather than physical. One day things come together and you're on top of the world. The next day things can fall apart and you're down."

Tim also mentioned this point one day, "When you're training animals, it will vary from day to day, simply because if things are going great one day and this animal gets a hind-leg walk and he's doing three steps in a row on the hind legs, you're like WOW!—then the next day he looks at you like I have no idea what you're asking me to do, you're like, 'Oh! I've failed.' That's one of those things in perspective, weeks from then you can see how that built up and it's just all part of it. The steps back are part of the steps forward."

Jim Cole commented on David's approach. "He's sensitive and sensible. He nails the basics down. Before the cats jump from a pedestal, they have to learn to sit on it. He teaches with the little bait stick, like Josip Marcan does. He holds the meat over their heads, and guides them up with the little crop whip. He uses their names. Calls them. And he doesn't scream at them."

Training Methods

David's philosophy is that "every animal can learn something. Some just take ten times longer." Once in the arena, the cats are trained through positive reinforcement. David uses meat as a reward. From the pouch on his belt he removes a golf-ball sized chunk of meat on a bamboo stick and offers it to a tiger to eat. David feeds some cats by hand. After a cat is trained, the meat and stick may be replaced by a flexible whip, which the cats see as an extension of the trainer's arms.

"Whip" sounds like a tool for punishment, but David corrected this false perception: "People have this image of a trainer using whips to train tigers. When I first train, I don't even use whips. I use a little bamboo stick or fiberglass rod to put the food on the end. But a whip flexes nicely, looks better in the act, and it's easier to carry around a six-ounce whip. The whips are used for direction and cues. But a whip certainly wouldn't hurt a cat or provide defense against an attack."

David doesn't use a whip for the first six months of training. "It's not a useful tool at that point. You can't cue cats very well with a whip at first because they want to play with it. I teased Shikar in the ring with a whip this morning, but I don't want them thinking it's playtime right away when I start a session."

5.3 David teaches the normally solitary tigers tolerance for each other as they practice the lay down.

Repetition, not force, is the key to control. David explained, "If you start hitting your cats they realize you're not that strong because you can't really hurt a cat. When they find out that you're just a weak human, they start to take advantage. These guys understand control is repeating the tricks." In later stages of training, the trainer's verbal approval becomes a substitute for food.

Communication

David communicates approval or displeasure with his voice tone. He said he could cuss them out in a soothing tone and they'd love it. But the typical words a modern trainer uses are "good" and "brav" followed by the cat's name to praise a desired behavior and "nyet" (Russian) and "no" to stop some potentially dangerous activity, such as jumping off the seat to roam and possibly fight with another cat. Sometimes voice tone is not enough. "If a cat messes up, a lot of times I'll chase him back to his seat, then right away make him sit up. Then you've got his attention. I started this disciplinary method on my own, then found out other trainers do it too."

David teaches the cats names for themselves, and for many objects and actions, such as "house," "here," "come here," "get over," "allez" (the French command for "go"), or "allez up" (for go up), "auf" (meaning 'on,' or 'on top of'), "roll over," "ho" for everybody to rise up. Bengal knows "back up" for the hind-leg walk; Prince knows "stand." Every trick has a word. David often talks to the cats in German "because it's a strong, precise language." A cat's seat or place is "platz"; David thinks the Russian "nyet" sounds better than "no"; and "brav" substitutes for "good."

Nancy said, "We have a lot of foreign visitors at the park. During the show we speak various phrases of Spanish and French. The cats know. It's more the intonation of your voice than actual language sometimes. But the foreign visitors love it when you say 'Mach schnell [move faster]!' "

Nancy recalled her own tiger training. "Communication is also nonverbal. In cueing any behavior, the trainer's or presenter's footsteps and walking patterns must be habitual. The animals need that security. Besides using your voice, you communicate with the animals through the position of the whip and your body movement. For example, you always approach them from the same side. To move differently, take a wrong step, or hold the whip differently can change the animals' response."

David said that nonverbal cues can be sufficient. "After a while you can drop the command word [for a behavior]; you just say their name and use body language." He boasted, "I made a bet one time that I could work cats a whole show with no commands, just body language. And I did." He was following in his father's footsteps. Larry had once performed his act in a Buster Keaton pantomime style.

David's training sessions vary in length depending on the number of cats in the ring: perhaps forty-five minutes for four or five cats and ten to fifteen minutes for just one cat. David usually limits his training with any one cat to one session per day, though he rarely misses a day once he decides to begin some trick or act.

He remarked, "The trainer can overdo it. If I'm in the ring twenty-five minutes with three tigers, that's enough. I get what I want done. Some guys say they've got to practice two to three times a day. The animals get broke faster, but are the animals stressed out, or angry?" David believes that patience pays in the long run. Once a cat has learned a trick, the animal remembers, so retraining is unnecessary even after time off (up to two years). The training time depends on many factors, especially the particular cat's tendencies and the experience of the trainer. David said that he's taught exceptional animals to sit up or roll over in just three or four days, while other cats took three to six months to learn to sit up. But progress was slower mostly when David was younger. He said, "Back then there were a lot of things I didn't know. Now if I can't teach a tiger to sit up in two weeks, I'm frustrated with myself, because I've learned better ways to do it."

Generally it now takes David twelve to sixteen months to train fresh cats and put an entire act together. But the process is complex. When I asked about the average time required to teach a tiger the lay down, David shook his head, "It really depends, because some will come out to the floor [where he wants them, instead of remaining on their seats]. You throw some meat down and they immediately lie down and stretch their paws out. I've had other cats—tigers or leopards—who will remain in the sitting position and just kneel or hunker down to take the meat and then sit right back up and not lie down.

"So for those you have to keep throwing the meat down, throwing the meat down. You could do that six to eight times in one practice and get nowhere. You have to work so long just to get them to lie down with their paws outstretched. Once they do that I really pour the meat on; I basically want them to be comfortable out in the middle of the ring so I just keep throwing the meat to keep their attention for about three or four minutes and if they get up to go away I tease them back with more meat or snap the whip [on the floor] to keep their attention."

David's Style Evolves

Besides presenting tricks which are known to please the crowd, David's act has changed in other ways as he has gained experience. As David summarized, "I've got a ways to go in this business. The day my dad passed away I only had seven leopards out there, and I wish he could have been there when I had seventeen."

At times David will eliminate something from the act, then due to popular demand, brings it back. He told me of one example, "For awhile I dropped Bengal going through the plastic hoop and everybody said, no it looks terrible [without that part of the act]—you got to have him do it again, so I brought that back in. Some days I'd as soon chop the hoop up in little pieces—just have him jump over me and Prince."

Acts may vary from one show to the next. David takes into account the animals' mood when he puts together which tricks will be in the day's act. Art Kozlik told me, "I've noticed that when David goes in the arena we never know what he's going to do [which tricks he will combine for the act]. The announcers have a basic script to follow, talking in general about tigers. But we don't tell the public what tricks David is going to do."

I was entertained by Art's description of his early days with David. "He and I used to have our spats. No doubt about that. The first three years I was working as groom I used to carry a pad and pencil [with me] every time he did a training session. Used to drive him crazy. I used to give a score of zero to ten. Every performance the cats would always get an eight or a nine. David's performance in the arena I used to give a zero, one, or two. 'Why?' he'd ask. 'You don't smile. No personality.' I always had the feeling David didn't care if anybody was watching the act, as long as he was accomplishing what he wanted to accomplish. Now, his presentation in the arena is a lot better than it ever was before. He's working the public. That's what you've got to do in show business. They're the ones that keep you in business."

Other Considerations

It's hard to get the cats to act together synchronously on command. David explained that "to teach one cat to lie down is nothing. I've seen the best acts in the world; whether it be Wade Burck or Gunther Gebel-Williams or Josip Marcan; the cats blow the lay down all the time; it's a lot more difficult than it looks. The biggest lay down I've done is only seven. James Clubb ribbed me that it doesn't get hard until you get over ten animals; then it gets tricky."

Like humans, cats are sometimes distracted and may be uncooperative. When I asked why Shikar wasn't in the lay down that particular day, David explained that the animal hadn't been paying attention lately, so "I just said the heck with it today. I want him to just sit there and get bored [in the arena, only watching] for a couple of days, then he'll want to work again."

Cat species vary. "Lions really like each other's company," David said. "If you look at any lion acts on tape, lions all come down and practically fall over each other just to lie down next to each other. They enjoy that, I believe, whereas tigers and leopards don't as much, so that's why I think it's technically more difficult to train a tiger than a lion to lie down."

The cat species also differ when they are in heat. "When tigers are in heat they still work well, unlike leopards or lions. When leopards come in heat, they're so miserable to be around. It's already hard enough to get them to pay attention."

Training leopards is very demanding partly because they are more hyper than the other cats. Groups of leopards are even worse, because they fight with each other at the least provocation. Even the most famous leopard trainers have managed only one or two complete leopard acts in their lives.

Training Specific Behaviors

Although David has invented some novel acts and techniques, most tricks are fairly standard. "Everyone's always trying to think up new stuff, or variations, but it's been a while since I've seen something new." Although David visits other acts in America or Europe, he rarely sees a new trick. Standard behaviors include lying down, sitting up, rolling over, and jumping through a hoop. While good trainers always teach these simpler behaviors, David said that many American acts are limited; for example, only some of the cats may sit up. On the other hand David said, "We [trainers] may be copying each other's work, but it's not like buying someone's animal pretrained [and simply presenting it]. Gunther is the only trainer besides me who had a leopard jump over another one on parallel ropes eight feet in the air. Once I trained two to do it," said David.

Trainers usually teach the repertoire of tricks in a particular order, beginning with sitting up and lying down. But first comes seat training.

Seat Training

Each animal is taught to go to its own place, and after each behavior to return to that same seat. The seat is an oversized stool, a steel pedestal about three feet high and twenty to twenty-two inches in diameter. Each animal's pedestal is always in about the same place in the arena. A seated tiger or leopard takes the same position as a house cat, with the back straight and angled to the vertical, and all four legs close together. In that position, the animal's seat fits him with a little room to spare.

No matter how long it takes, seat breaking is the first thing to build on. David explained, "A seat-broken cat is a plus for a trainer, because no matter what goes wrong, he knows those cats better be on their seats. For instance, it's important in rare cases when a cat in a cranky mood jumps off his seat and approaches another cat. Because the trainer knows the others will stay on their seats, he can devote his attention to the misbehaving cat [who could cause a crisis]. To the cat his seat is a security position." Usually other cats won't bother him, and trainers rarely discipline an animal on his seat.

5.4 David seat-training five leopards.

"It takes more confidence to get tigers up on props than leopards. Tigers are more comfortable on the ground. That's why most leopard acts you'll see use a lot more pedestal tricks than floor tricks.

"In seat-breaking, I'll toss a piece of meat onto a seat. When the cat takes the meat, he will be rewarded with my voice and an additional snack. Eventually they know that seat is theirs and my voice and attention will be their reward."

David explained how one trick progresses to other behaviors. "Gradually, he's coming on cue to you and going back. A good trainer basically trains the cat to come, and won't drive him off the seat [as trainers of decades ago routinely did]." When the cat is on the floor in the ring, David can train other behaviors.

The Sit-up

When a seated cat sits up, he balances on his rear legs and lifts his front paws in front of him to head level. His back is straight and vertical, and his front and rear legs are nearly so.

5.5 David rehearsing the leopard and panther sit-up.

David teaches cats to sit up one animal at a time. The cat may remain seated on his own pedestal, where he is most comfortable. Just as a dog owner might do, David holds the meat (on a stick) above the animal's head, so it has to sit up for the treat.

The trainer uses the whip (as a tickler or distraction) above the cat's face and front paws, to lengthen the sitting time somewhat. After repeated practice sessions, the time period gradually increases, until the cat sits up only with the whip as a pointer sweeping upward, often with David saying "allez up," "ho," or "sit up."

When performing, the cat has to concentrate while sitting up on a twenty-two-inch-square pedestal top that's five feet in the air. Since he's used to being in the open on the ground, he has to learn his balance and overcome his fear. "That's why I often start sitting a cat up on a very low pedestal (about eighteen-inch-high) then gradually raise that height." Suppressing a smile, David said, "By the time they learn the trick they can sit up on the moon or wherever."

From her experience training tigers, Nancy explained the difficulty of getting the cats to come from their seats and stay in one place out in the arena. "When you throw the meat down the first thing they want to do is just stand there and eat the meat. Then you give them another piece. Most of them will then sit and eat and look for another piece. Then you can gradually back up and drop the next piece out a little farther, so they gradually come down. Then you start the praising. You're giving the cue 'down' all the while. When you get them into position, you softly praise, 'Good, good, good,' then 'hold, hold, hold.' You try to get them to stay there while you walk around the arena. That takes awhile, because they're always watching you and tend to follow. So you say something like, 'Down, stay, stay, good, good.' But it's difficult because when they're out in the arena they feel very vulnerable. They have cats behind them and you moving around, so they have to do a lot of trusting. Some cats take longer than others, even to leave their seats."

When I first observed David's act five years ago, I was moved to see several cats sitting up at once, with their movements in harmony and their postures maintained for some seconds. Although unified acts need considerable practice, the transition from separate to simultaneous behaviors is easier for the trainer to teach once the cats perform individually on the trainer's cue (such as the upward sweeping motion of the whip for sitting up).

The Lay Down

The next behavior a trainer usually tackles is the lay down. In this posture, the cat lies on her belly with hind legs folded under and front legs extended. This looks impressive when several animals closely spaced, side by side, perform the movements at the same time. Using meat as a reward, the trainer first encourages the cats to come from their respective seats and sit several inches apart, though not so close that they tend to fight. Like humans, the big cats need personal space.

The trainer tries to get the seated cats to lie down by dropping meat far enough in front of them that they either must get up and walk forward or else stretch out, and in the process, lie down. Although progress is gradual, David said that it's just a matter of perseverance. "You keep dropping the food and each day you spread out the time when you drop the food. So they just learn to sit there and wait and they know it's going to come sooner or later. At the same time, when you're throwing the food, you keep talking to them—calling their name, telling them the name of the trick."

Although leopards are harder to train than tigers, one exception is the rollover. Leopards work on their backs more easily than tigers, because it's the leopard's fighting position. David said that tigers feel uncomfortable on their backs; they fight that way only as a last resort. On the other hand, getting leopards to roll over in groups is a challenge because they feel uncomfortable together (and tend to fight).

The Rollover

David teaches his cats to roll over on the floor, a complete 360-degree turn. Usually several cats lined up on the arena floor turn through three complete revolutions. David said he's trained at least eleven leopards to roll over, as well as one lion and seven tigers. Most tiger acts have at least one cat doing the rollover. David likes to go beyond the basics. But first he teaches them one by one.

I asked David, because he'd handled the leopards since they were cubs, would he begin teaching the rollover by manually rolling them over, then rewarding them? He immediately said, "Never! First they have to be comfortable, lying on their sides, with their legs out. Some you can tease sideways with a whip; they look over their shoulder at it. You need to touch them on their shoulder or their hip."

5.6 An amazing seven-leopard rollover!

Nancy adds that although tigers naturally roll over as cubs, they seem to forget when they're in the arena. One of the hardest things is to teach a tiger to roll over. She explained her technique, which differs from David's. "I use two sticks and meat. If they're sitting down, I get them to lie over on their sides, then give them praise and meat. I maneuver with the piece of meat to get them to follow me, and they roll over. Sometimes they look at me like, 'What happened?' or they get back to where they were and seem to express, 'What did I do?' Some adapt easily and others are uncomfortable because on their backs and rolling over they feel unprotected. You teach them to roll over individually, then when you get two together, that's when you get problems because one is afraid the other's going to attack him (and sometimes does)."

Most trainers roll over one or two animals. James Clubb taught four leopards to roll over. Gunther Gebel-Williams typically rolled over five or six. David did five or more.

Many trainers combine these various tricks in a single act. But unlike other acts that have leopards roll over one after another, David's spotted leopards rolled over simultaneously. I thought it spectacular to see all the white bellies up at once. David's act is also distinctive because he has developed harder, infrequently performed tricks.

Jumping Using Pedestals, Hoops, and Arms

To get big cats to jump, David first gets them to step across two seat-high pedestals, with meat on one. Then he works toward a short jump. He's had some animals, mostly tigers, walk across the pedestals for a week before they'll jump.

Unlike leopards, tigers usually avoid heights. David said, "I've had a few tigers who just love to jump and will do it all day long and others get up on a pedestal five feet high and they get such odd facial expressions it's like they think they're sitting on top of Mount McKinley." Leopards easily learn to jump, because they're arboreal, or tree animals. A leopard can jump five feet the first day.

Once a cat learns to jump from low to high pedestals and back again, David teaches the animal to jump through a hoop he holds above his head. David said that it's easy to train a tiger to jump through a hoop. "Although they may not like to, most tigers can learn to jump easily. Some tigers can initially do short jumps; others have to begin by stepping across pedestals. A tiger knows he's a heavy animal and needs a solid landing. Once reassured of a solid landing, the tiger cooperates. When a tiger can jump well, I reverse the training; I shorten the jump, and start holding the hoop there."

When I interviewed David, he was training an eighteen-month-old tiger named India to do this trick. An adult tiger, Bengal, had been doing the hoop trick for years. Eventually David would like to have India follow Bengal through the hoop.

He has trained leopards to jump to his arms. The first time it happened was a surprise to David. A spotted leopard, Honey, spontaneously jumped to David's arms. Honey was taught to stand on her hind legs and hug David. During one performance, Honey became overzealous in her nuzzling and jumped to David's arms and licked his face. Thinking this a neat trick, David used treats to encourage Honey to continue. "When I had Honey jump to my arms, I thought it was original. Later I discovered George Koran, in France, had done that trick first."

Later David taught a black leopard, Ebony, to jump from a pedestal to his arms. "I placed meat first on one pedestal then on another and started touching Ebony as she landed. Pretty soon, she leapt to the pedestal, but then I grabbed her just before she got there; after a while she knew she'd have a safe landing on me instead of the pedestal."

5.7 David and Missy perform the shoulder-carry, one of the most difficult behaviors.

Draping a Leopard Over Shoulders

Draping a 120-pound cat around his shoulders was a trick that took David six months to perfect in 1984. "Almost every big-time leopard act has a shoulder-carry. I haven't seen one that doesn't. Some trainers use declawed animals to do this trick, but I don't. I trained two that rode on my shoulders perfectly, and two that were borderline. The two perfect ones took about six months each," he said.

"I trained the behavior in two different ways. I taught Missy, a black leopard, to stretch across two pedestals, front feet on one pedestal and back feet on another; I'd put the meat on the front pedestal. Then I'd duck under when she went for the meat. I'd push up on her stomach a little, then more and more, then finally I'd take a couple of steps. With Dusty, I carried her in my arms right in front of me, for about four months; then I'd start bouncing her up, up, then I lifted her over my shoulders. That's how they do it in England, where I got the idea. Both methods worked; each took about the same amount of time to train."

Shoulder Stand

In the fall of 1992 David taught the sixteen-month old tiger, Nirvana, to stand on her hind legs and put her front paws on his shoulders putting them nose-to-nose. He started training Nirvana to do this when she was about 150 pounds. As she becomes full grown, despite her size, she will still be able to do this trick.

It is a matter of trial and error to find a cat who is good for this type of contact—one that you can hand feed who trusts the trainer. At first you have to show them where to put their paws once they stand up.

Sitting on a Tiger

In another trick the crowds enjoy, David straddles Prince, a five hundred-pound tiger, as he would mount a horse. In the act, David holds his arms high to encourage applause. Then David holds a hoop high overhead for Bengal. The 550-pound, full-grown male jumps through a hoop from a lower to higher pedestal, and then back from the higher to lower one. David said, "You don't see that in every act—a trainer sitting on a tiger, holding a hoop and having another tiger jump through that. You'll see someone holding a hoop and maybe even standing beside another tiger, but not sitting on a tiger."

In training for this unusual trick, David first had Prince stand on low pedestals, then on successively higher ones as he became more confident.

5.8 The "mouse" that roared—David astride Prince.

Then David had to work on sitting on Prince. David explained how this tiger allowed him this close physical contact; "I taught Prince to stand on pedestals, then spent a few weeks just standing next to him, then leaning on his back, then standing behind him, then sitting on his rear, with pressure on his back.

"After about a month I sat on his shoulders. If I had tried to sit on him the first day, I would have been bitten. A trainer has to earn the animal's confidence."

Hind-leg Walking

David has trained more than five hind-leg walkers. "Some people didn't train any in their whole careers so I guess I'm lucky. Hind-leg walking is a touchy thing." David said, "That's the one thing I was taught by someone else. I'm one of no more than four or five people in the world who knows this method. That's why you don't see that many hind-leg walking cats. People haven't found a standard method for it. I was taught in secret by a great trainer, Jim Clubb. Before that I'd seen other people work on hind-leg walks, and I had already trained three hind-leg-walking cats. So far I've used Clubb's method to train hind-leg walking once and it worked very well for that cat."

David speculates that Clubb passed on his methods out of respect for David and his desire to help continue to be an asset to the profession. "Clubb has trained more hind-leg-walking cats than anybody because he has this superior method. I've trained one leopard to walk using his method and I'll probably train some tigers to do it too. But if I were a trainer in Europe, Clubb wouldn't have told me, because then I would have been competition."

Tigers are a more natural hind-leg-type animal than leopards because tigers fight on their hind legs. Leopards do to an extent, but not much.

5.9 Java hind-leg walks with David. (photo courtesy of David Jamieson)

David has presented several variants of hind-leg walking. The animal can walk forward, hop forward, walk backward, or spin in a circle, like Centaine does.

A Few Failures

Despite his tenacity, David has had to give up on a trick, but never an entire act. For example, once David tried to get a leopard to jump through a paper hoop, but she kept jumping over the hoop, not through it, so he dropped the trick.

David can sometimes turn failures into successes. "Some years ago I acquired two nine- or ten-month-old Siberian tiger cubs and the first day I went into the cage they tried to chase me out. I couldn't get near them, couldn't pet them. They were so hostile, it took two weeks to get them to take meat off a stick. It wasn't anything I did. They were mother-raised and she taught them to be snots, which is natural. But the fact that I did train them and they turned into good animals was exciting for me because until I worked with those two guys, I'd only worked with animals I or someone else had hand raised."

5.10 Dusty, an Indian leopard, uses David as "a stepping stone."

Unique Tricks

During his career, David has developed several unusual tricks such as the stepping stone which he did with leopards. While

David leaned over and put his hands on his knees, one leopard named Dusty crossed the arena by leaping from one pedestal to a higher one, to David's back to two subsequent pedestals. In effect, David was part of the arena equipment. For years David used a leather vest for that trick with the leopard. He went through a lot of vests before the leopard quit sticking her claws out. David then did the act with the leopard jumping on his polo-shirt-covered back.

Another of David's special tricks was the leopard blanket. After teaching the leopards to lie down, David made himself part of their "blanket." Here's how it worked: In the act, David went to the center of the arena and sat down. He called the lead cat, Ben, to come forward and lie down next to or on top of David. Four other leopards came from their seats forward to surround David, creating the "blanket."

"Only Gunther Gebel-Williams and Dickie Chipperfield have also done this trick. In his version, Dickie actually used a cat for a pillow, while Gunther and I used one for a 'backrest' while the other cats were on our legs and beside us," said David.

5.11 David relaxes under the leopard "blanket."

David also had eight leopards on the "stretch bar." For this trick a bar is placed on pedestals about three-and-one-half feet off the floor across the arena. David called the leopards forward to balance on their hind legs, with their front paws on the bar.

"That is difficult. Jim Clubb told me that Alfred Court is the only other one who ever put eight on the bar," said David. "Court even had ten spotted leopards over the stretch bar," he said. David also taught seven leopards to walk across ropes eight feet off the ground. About one in ten big cats will consent to walk across the bars—the preliminary for teaching rope walking. The animals walk across bars just a few feet off the ground. Then the bars get raised; then the bars are replaced with ropes.

5.12 Two pairs of tigers go "over the garden wall."

When teaching the "over-the-garden-wall" trick David saw spontaneous success—the tigers performed the trick perfectly during a performance for the first time instead of during training. This delighted him and his back-ups, but the audience thought it was David's usual, wonderful performance. One of his back-ups, Becky Speer, talked about the moment of success. "David was teaching the two tiger cubs India and Nirvana the trick. Nirvana lays down with paws outstretched in front of her and India walks over and sits on her, facing the audience with her paws in the air. One day he decided to try it during the show to see if it would work and they did it right away—like WOW!—and he and

I had big smiles on our faces, but the audience didn't have a clue. We were working for months on that, and all of a sudden it clicked." David especially likes this trick, because he said no one does that with cats except Jim Clubb and Karoly Donnert. But he has improved on the act to include two pairs of tigers performing this trick simultaneously, one pair on either side of the arena's center.

Teaching the cats to perform tricks is just part of the trainer's work. He also must fashion acts from individual behaviors, familiarize the cats with the sequences, relieve or replace animals with substitutes, and make other adjustments. As Ovid wrote, "Ars est celare artem." Translated, the saying means, "The art is to conceal the art." Those words of wisdom apply to the skill of the tiger trainer when presenting his animals to the public.

"People like the animal act and the behaviors I've trained the animals to do, but sometimes I think I make it look too easy. The audience doesn't know the sweat I put into this," said David.

5.13 A big kiss at the end of the day makes it all worth it!

One of the trainer's decisions is whether to begin teaching cats singly or together, and when to bring them into a group. One-on-

one contact with an animal is generally easier. In a group, the trainer must have more distance between himself and the animals (to be able to see them all at once) and he needs to be more alert. But the animals must come together at some point, either after they know the individual tricks or before.

David changes his strategy to fit the situation and animals. Sometimes he puts cubs with adult tigers who know the tricks and sequences. I have seen him teach baby tigers the rollover independently, as a group, and with an adult tiger. David said it's not always easier if you have a lead cat who knows the tricks. "It depends. Wade Burck [a tiger trainer with Ringling Circus] had a big male tiger, Tony, who was always the lead cat for the lay down. But although the lead cat may be the one that all the other tigers respect, that doesn't always help the other cats learn any faster. Just because the babies [India, Nirvana, and Shikar] see Bengal and Centaine lay down, they're not necessarily going to come and lie down beside them."

David said that once the cats know their individual behaviors, training a sequence is not hard. "They have to get to know what's coming. Usually I'll start that when I'm teaching them the tricks. If the adult tigers already know the sequence of tricks, I just put the cubs in that situation. So they learn that the pedestal tricks come first and then we do things on the floor."

Altering the sequence of behaviors or changing the music accompaniment causes few problems, although a major change in a routine of several years can take the cats a little while to get used to. The positioning of the props cues them to what they're supposed to do.

Nancy commented on changing sequences. "Usually before David starts training, he has a plan of what he wants the finished act to look like, but in the ten years he's been doing the leopard act, he's sometimes changed the order. If he feels the cats are getting a little bored with doing the same thing, he'll change the act around to get their attention again. It also helps David to stay fresh and not become too routine."

Another stage of act development is having new animals, who have been trained independently, join an established act. New members join when the act is made larger or, less often, when a cat is temporarily sick, is pregnant or being given a break from the routine. If an animal refuses to work or gets too old, it is retired, usually in a spacious area on the Naples grounds, with other members of its own species.

When adding animals to the act, the trainer needs extra patience and concentration. The young ones may be familiar with a small group they've practiced with, but don't always immediately know what's expected of them when they're put with the older animals. Smiling, David said, "Meanwhile, the others [adults] screw me up because they know I'm watching the new cat and not them."

In 1992 David added the three young animals, India, Nirvana, and Shikar, to his already impressive act. As with the very successful leopard act David had, he plans to build the tiger act by adding animals. India and Nirvana's introduction to the tiger act went much easier than if there had been leopard cubs being introduced to mature leopards. "But the older ones tried to take advantage today. They often tried to get off their seats, so I had to get them right back up. Leopards, because of their nature, can be all over the place, climbing the side of the cage, messing with other leopards." Although tigers aren't like that, they need more space to travel in the arena, so David will probably stop at eight tigers in the act.

Besides the main performers, acts also need back-up cats. David feels the regulars should be pulled periodically to allow them a break before they get burned out. David is aware that overwork, particularly with hind-leg walking, can injure animals. "I had two hind-leg-walking leopards because I don't want to burn anybody out. A lot of trainers use an animal too much," David said sadly. "I don't want to look back and say I crippled this animal for my own ego. If an animal starts to have trouble I'll stop it." That is difficult, though, because not every tiger will routinely walk on his hind legs or every leopard be carried on your neck. On the other hand, David trained nine leopards to roll over and normally used four or five of them in the show.

Final Results

Tim said, "I've heard about a lot of different trainers that go through many, many cats before they decide a particular cat can do this behavior, this one can do that. And I've seen acts with seven or eight cats that don't do as many behaviors as Dave did when he had a troupe of three."

David is particularly proud of his early leopard act. "The problems with leopards come when you try to put them together, because of their personality conflicts. It's just so hard to get them down on the ground and stay there and roll over three times to-

104   Living with Big Cats

gether. It's really difficult. So most leopard acts just do one or two rolling over.

"You have to space them just right so they don't bump into each other. In the many leopard acts and various videos I've seen [and he's seen a lot] the animals were two or three feet apart and they rolled over individually, not together. Even Gunther's leopard rollovers were like that. But I had five, six, and seven spaced closely together." David sounded wistful when he told me, "This

sounds cocky, but I had an excellent five-spotted-leopard rollover and to me, that rollover was the best one, because they all rolled at the same time, white bellies up, synchronized and they were all practically touching each other. They were very, very close."

PART TWO

Larry and Nancy Jane undertook something
that is quite remarkable among animal people.
They started a show and a park and
they succeeded . . . quite spectacularly!
—Frank Thompson, former zoo director

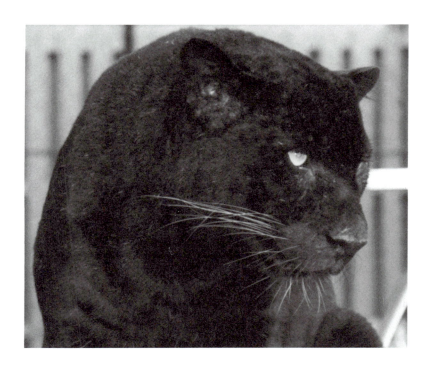

6

Learning from Jungle Larry

At eighteen, Larry was acknowledged by renowned herpetologist and author Raymond L. Ditmar, as the world's youngest herpetologist. He was in demand by schools and colleges for lectures, and all kinds of civic groups to demonstrate snake handling and milking.   —Nancy Jane

DAVID TETZLAFF had the best teacher to lead him into his career as an animal trainer—his world-famous father, Jungle Larry. While other boys were playing baseball or building forts, David was living with big cats, and learning how to care for and train them.

The park in Naples, where David spent much of his youth, was the culmination of Larry's dream. This dream included his dedication to the care and breeding of wild animals. It all started, however, with Larry's fascination with the snakes he caught as a kid in Kalamazoo, Michigan. Before he was eleven years old, Larry had collected approximately 250 snakes.

As Larry's younger brother, Rique von Tetzlaff (Rique restored the "von" to the family name) recalls, Larry would go almost daily to a stream in the nearby woods. He was intrigued by anything that crawled, flew, or jumped. Larry continually brought snakes home, using a forked stick to pick up the snakes, and transfer them to his canvas bag. Before church on Sunday mornings he would go to the creek to find frogs to feed his snakes.

Rique worked with Larry on his early lecture tours with live reptiles, billed as "Teaching the truth, not myth, about reptiles." In 1979, after retiring from his career in the fashion world, Rique rejoined his brother's business in Naples, and even now continues to work part-time in the Jungle Larry's gift shop. He described for me what his brother was like as a young man.

Rique speculated that Larry's love of animals came from his father, who was a contractor who loved the circus. Whenever the circus came to town, their father would take Larry down at five or six in the morning to watch the tent go up. Larry's father also built numerous cages for the growing snake collec-

6.1 Rique (left) and Larry (right) with their father, George Tetzlaff, holding one of their snakes.

tion. Rique said that in the early days "neighbors and town people were curious about the snakes and would flock to our house to see them. When Larry had acquired some 250 reptiles, he opened a back-yard attraction called Larry's Trained Snakes, with a fifteen-cent admission charge.

"When he was twelve years old and I was ten, Larry heard there were Massasauga rattlesnakes in the woods outside of town. So we packed our camping gear to go there for two nights. It turned out to be mosquito woods. To get away from the mosquitoes, we spent most of the night in the water. The next morning I hitchhiked the twenty miles back to town, but Larry loved the place and stayed two days. However, he did not see one rattlesnake. If they'd been there, Larry would have found them."

This was the beginning of Larry's career with animals—a vocation demanding intense communication with animals and people. Young Larry excelled at everything—sports, track, baseball.

In 1937, Larry had so many snakes that his collection had outgrown the cage system his father had built, so eighteen-year-old Larry approached the city of Kalamazoo about leasing an old log cabin in Milham Park for his exhibit. The city fathers agreed and his exhibit remained there through the summer of 1938. By then, Larry's collection had outgrown the log cabin! The Kilgores, a local family, had a vacant corner lot on their farm facing Milham Park. The Kilgores were so impressed with Larry's dedication and research on reptiles that they allowed him to build the Tetzlaff Reptilium on their property.

Even through the Depression, Larry made a living with his exhibits, at first by soliciting circuses that came to Kalamazoo. But later the carnivals and circuses sought him out to buy reptiles. In 1936, Larry's opinion was solicited on a reptile's health. Ripley's traveling exhibit came through Kalamazoo and the manager looked up seventeen-year-old Larry to inspect a twenty-five-foot python's severely infected mouth. Rique recalled, "Larry cleaned out the snake's mouth. He had never done anything like that before, but he saved the snake's life."

6.2 The Reptilium in Kalamazoo, where Larry began his career.

Rique continued, "One incident I'll never forget: We had all these poisonous snakes, large water moccasins, and one was pregnant and ready to shed her skin. Larry was afraid he'd lose the babies. He'd never had any before. He wanted to help conserve her energy by helping her shed her skin—just peel it away from her nose so she could get it started. I was holding the body and he was holding the head until it slipped. Larry was bitten five times in one hand. Even though he was in excruciating pain, he threw the snake back into the cage and slammed the door to protect me. He was rushed to the hospital where he was given the antivenin." The snakes were born a couple of weeks later. Mother moccasin, babies, and Larry all survived.

6.3 Jungle Larry holding Australian pythons.

With earnings from the summer exhibits in Kalamazoo, Larry paid tuition at the University of Michigan where he studied herpetology. In 1938 he wrote a groundbreaking scholarly paper titled, "Keeping Snakes Alive in Captivity," suggesting ways to decrease the high mortality rate of imported snakes in captivity.

Frank "Bring 'Em Back Alive" Buck, the most famous big game hunter of that time, obtained a copy of Larry's paper and, impressed with Larry's ideas, phoned to offer him a job. Instead of enrolling for another semester, Larry dropped out of college in 1939 to work with Buck at his Amity, Long Island, import/export facility. Larry, caring for Buck's snakes, cut their death rate from fifty percent to almost zero. Within a year, twenty-year-old Larry was put in charge of Buck's reptile collection. He spent three years learning from Buck how to handle everything from anteaters to zebras.

It was during his tenure with Frank Buck that Larry was nicknamed "Jungle Larry." Nancy explained that "When Larry was with Buck, a German gentleman started calling him 'Jhungle Larrrry.' In the late 1940s and early 1950s, Jungle Larry was a natural name since other TV personalities were called Captain Penny, Captain Kangaroo, and Uncle Jake." After the nickname caught on, his friends used to kid him, "Hi, Jungle." Others who didn't know him actually thought Jungle was Larry's first name!

The name went with Larry's public character of a safari man in hat and boots. But wearing a hat was more than an image as Nancy revealed. "Larry learned early in life that a hat can save your life. When Larry was exploring in the jungles, several times a snake dropped from a tree and struck only his hat."

From Tarzan to The Classroom

Larry achieved a worldwide reputation as a knowledgeable, compassionate animal caretaker, Nancy Jane told me. At age twenty-one he managed the Oldest City Alligator Ranch and Ostrich Farm, in St. Augustine, Florida, where he daily wrestled ten- to twelve-foot alligators. Later in the 1940s, Larry began training lions with Captain Fred Marx, in St. Augustine. Then for one or two years he was superintendent of the Florida Wild Animal and Reptile Ranch at St. Petersburg. Later Larry worked at Ross Allen's Alligator Farm at Silver Springs, Florida—again, wrestling alligators and milking snakes.

In the 1940s Larry got a job on the Tarzan set in Silver Springs. Larry was responsible for the care of all the film crew's exotic animals and prepared them for the scenes. He did the underwater stunt work with the alligators (referred to as crocodiles in these films). To help cameramen set up, Larry went through the action scenes before Johnny Weissmuller actually performed them. Larry appeared as a stand-in in the picture, *Tarzan Finds a Son,* eventually working with Weissmuller on three Tarzan films.

Larry worked in dozens of other movies, either wrestling pythons, alligators, or lions or serving as a stuntman with elephants and tigers. He also starred in two movies of his own—*Anaconda* and *Spotted Killer*. Larry produced several educational films compiled from his safari footage: *Vanishing Everglades* (Florida), *Safari Across the Earth* (Australia), *Brightest East Africa* (Kenya).

6.4 Jungle Larry demonstrates how to handle an American alligator.

Milking Snakes for One's Country

Because of a snake bite in 1940 that required Larry to wear a permanent leg brace, he was exempt from combat service during WW II. His service was not that of the typical soldier, but his skills were put to good use. He caught rattlesnakes in Texas and Florida and milked them for the army to make antivenin serum for soldiers bitten in the jungles of the South Pacific. Cottonmouth venom helped coagulate blood; cobra venom sometimes reduced night blindness. Nancy told me that Larry ended up milking one-quarter million rattlesnakes during the war.

After the army had enough venom, they found another job for Larry, drawing on his experience as a volunteer St. Petersburg firefighter. Larry became a "hot poppa"—so called because of the job of extinguishing airplane fires. At MacDill Air Force Base in Tampa Larry rescued pilots from crashed planes.

During 1942 to 1945, when he was in the service, Larry lost his contacts for the animal business. So when he became a civilian, he moved from Michigan to Ohio and managed the Muir Drugstore in Lorain, Ohio. For a few years he worked there full time while again building up his animal contacts and making a few TV appearances.

Early TV and the Educational Circuit

Around 1949, Larry began doing TV guest spots on various children's shows, mostly for Channel 5 in Cleveland, Ohio. He was on many popular TV shows: "Pooch Parade," "Mary Ellen's Fun Farm," and Gene Carroll's "Uncle Jake Show." Then Larry started on the longest-running local children's show, the "Captain Penny Show," where he appeared regularly for eighteen years (1951 to 1969). Larry was a guest on many other TV shows throughout his career.

Nancy said, "All those years he was on TV he was never paid. It was strictly a way to promote our summer locations or the money raisers we had coming up."

Larry would load his yellow station wagon or his zebra-striped van with reptiles and other wild animals and travel over a three-state area to give lectures and ever-popular shows at schools. Central High School's auditorium, the school from which Larry had graduated two decades earlier, was filled to its 2,500 capacity for one of Larry's presentations.

For elementary and high school lectures, Larry showed and narrated a thirty-minute film. After the film, Larry presented an exhibit of exotic birds and animals on stage. When he went into the classroom and the teacher introduced Larry as Mr. Tetzlaff, the kids would shout, "No that isn't. It's Jungle Larry!" Nancy laughed. "Larry was so popular that even the truants would show up, because it was a unique assembly program—they saw the film and live animals."

"Safari Jane" Joins the Act

The summer day in 1957 when nineteen-year-old, hazel-eyed, Nancy Rose Gettling met thirty-eight-year-old Jungle Larry was action-packed. It started near the cougar cage and ended with

Nancy having her picture taken with a huge boa constrictor draped over her bare shoulders.

6.5 Safari Jane wrapped in a reticulated python.

Nancy was working at Mutual Boiler Insurance and spent many evenings roller skating at Puritas Springs Park in Cleveland. "One summer afternoon in August 1957," she told me, "I took my younger brother around the park which had a roller rink on the edge of a valley. Larry happened to come to my high school assembly in 1955, and I'd liked his show, so my brother and I went through his exhibit.

"Larry had a South American cougar, José, who detested men. He'd growl, hiss, and swipe his paws whenever a man would pass his cage. He was likely captured by a man and mistreated during the capture. I had always loved animals and I knelt down in front of the cougar's cage and quietly said, 'José, what a beautiful creature you are!' He started purring. Larry stopped when he heard the cat purring and introduced himself.

"That same day, not knowing I was deathly afraid of snakes, Larry brought out a snake for people to pet. Larry saw my camera and asked if I'd like a picture. I didn't know that he meant with the snake on my shoulders. I was wearing a playsuit with straps. He put the snake on me. An employee of his took a picture of me screaming with a boa constrictor on my bare skin! Larry became extremely apologetic and lifted the snake off me, then very softly talked me through the fear. After a short time, he put it back on my shoulders and got a picture of me smiling and that was the end of my fear of snakes. I went back another day because Larry was so interesting to talk to; he asked me out to dinner August 8, 1957.

6.6 Nancy's parents, Gertrude and Lew Gettling.

"As I became closer to Larry, I got to know José. José would let me walk him on a leash. He'd sit on my lap and purr, then Larry would come near and José would hiss. The first time Larry approached unannounced I panicked, thinking how José might react, but the aggression was never aimed at me—only men. Once while Larry was filling a pail with drinking water for the animals, he turned his back to José's cage, thinking the door was shut. José silently stole up to Larry and with one swipe of his paw ripped out the seat of Larry's khaki pants. In May, about nine months after I entered Larry's life, the cougar's attitude toward Larry finally changed. Larry told me delightedly, 'José let me pet him!' It was a triumph for us to overcome that cat's hatred of men.

"I would help Larry weekends while I worked at the insurance office. After meeting him in August, we were married December 1, 1957 with Ron Penfound [Captain Penny] as our best man. We started out life together in a very primitive, furnitureless, log cabin in Vermilion, Ohio. My dad volunteered to take care of our animals so we could have a two and one-half-day honeymoon. At that time, our animals would fit in a single-car garage: one lioness, a cougar, monkeys, baboon, alligator, birds, a vulture, snakes, lion hunting dogs, sloths, agoutis, and kinkajous.

"Animal training came with Larry. 'Love me, love my animals.'" Nancy's eyes sparkled as she recalled, "You couldn't be married to Larry and not share his life. Can you imagine being nineteen years old and this man that loves you has married you and has this wonderful way of life with all these magnificent creatures! I felt like a princess on an adventure."

Nancy said she went to the "Tetzlaff University." Larry bragged to friends that Nancy, at twenty-one, picked up in a couple of years most of the knowledge it had taken him a lifetime to learn.

Before meeting Nancy, Larry worked with a man he called Safari Jack. One weekend the two men were to do a promotion at a shopping center. The shopping center furnished a flatbed trailer to use as the performing stage. In the full-page newspaper ad someone mistakenly printed that Jungle Larry and Safari Jane were coming, printing "Jane" instead of "Jack." After that, the Tetzlaffs decided Nancy would be "Safari Jane." She later changed her legal name to Nancy Jane Tetzlaff.

"My first public appearance was on a stage at the Toledo Zoo just six weeks after meeting Larry. It was Appreciation Day for the zoo members, with over 10,000 people in the audience. Instead of calling me Safari Jane, the announcer introduced me as Jungle Mary!" recalled Nancy.

For their first shows in the late 1950s, rather than having trained animals perform, the Tetzlaffs presented animals in what is called contact work. At various places—like the Toledo Zoo—Jungle Larry and Safari Jane worked on an open stage, carrying animals on-stage or bringing them on leash to show them to the audience and talk about the species. Nancy told me about the early shows. "Larry was in the center of the stage and I took a reptile, like an eight- to ten-foot boa, out of the cage and carried it to the front. After Larry's demonstration, I'd take the snake back to its cage.

"I would go in José's cage, put him on my lap, and lecture about cougars. Larry and I showed how movies produce the visual effect of cats attacking people. Two of Larry's four show lions were also trained to wrestle for movies and TV. We put a hunk of raw meat on Larry's chest, and had a lion eat the meat, making it look as if Larry was being attacked."

Through the years Nancy has worked with just about any animal that could be handled. She has arm-trained a king vulture named Bonita, that they acquired when it was young. "Bonita had a ring around her leg and a short chain and leash, so I could bait her to come up on my arm. I went out in the audience with her. For positive reinforcement—again, contact work—I'd put a raw chicken heart between my teeth and she'd gently take it out of my mouth and eat it. I guess I'm lucky I didn't get salmonella doing that.

6.7 Safari Jane with her Indian leopards, Smokey and Amber.

"Once I did a TV show while Larry stayed at home at Chippewa Lake compound. The next day he went down to open the building and check on the animals. Some people walked by and said, 'Oh, that's Safari Jane's husband.' He came up to the cottage beaming, 'You made it! I'm Safari Jane's husband!' He was so proud."

Their early acts included Larry's four lions, cougars, birds, a king vulture and harmony acts—performances exhibiting species that are natural enemies working congenially together. One of Larry's harmony acts featured the unlikely combo of chimp, llama, and reptile. Larry liked to combine animals that usually did not even reside on the same continent. For example, chimpanzees prefer a hot, humid, tropical rain forest. Llamas, from South America, prefer the cold in the dry, windy mountains.

Larry's Lions

Besides reptiles, Larry's animal love was lions. Larry began his lion act by acquiring Sheba in 1956. By 1960, Larry had two lions he had trained to perform in both humorous and serious shows. In his humorous shows, Jungle Larry told a lion to sit on his stool. The lion ignored him. Larry gave the command again, pointing to the lion's seat. The lion just stood there. "Sit," he repeated louder. Still nothing. "I said sit!" he yelled. The lion sauntered over and sat on the stool. "See how quickly he obeys," Larry said to the amused audience, who had each paid fifty cents to see the show. "Okay, now shake hands," Jungle Larry said. The lion snarled at Larry and swept his paw in front of Larry. He jumped back, "I said **shake** hands, not **take** hands!"

6.8 Larry nose-to-nose with one of the tiglon triplets.

For the serious performances, Larry had the lions do basic tricks such as jumps, sit-ups, lay downs, rollovers, and contact work. "Larry could cue this same act in three styles: comedy or Buster Keaton style, Clyde Beatty style, and his own style—similar to what David does today," Nancy said. "Larry shuffled like

Buster Keaton, cueing them through the whole act. That style was performed silently, with exaggerated gestures, to the music from silent movies. He could also work the cats Clyde Beatty style, with the circus music and whip cracking, again over-exaggerating the movements, like when Clyde Beatty acted with cats that seemed vicious. For that style Larry put his head in a lion's mouth, too. For any style, the cats would respond perfectly, because it was the same trainer and cues; only Larry's movements were different."

Safaris and Conservation

Larry and Nancy made numerous trips to South America, Africa, and the Caribbean. Larry's animal-capturing safaris and personally-guided jungle tours added to his international reputation. In twenty-seven years, he traveled on ten safaris. After Nancy and Larry married, she wanted to go on safari with him.

Nancy recalled that in September of 1958, Larry fulfilled his dream of going to Australia, where there are more poisonous snakes than nonpoisonous varieties. "Larry brought back the largest collection of reptiles ever permitted to leave Australia. When he got home, he shipped the reptiles to the zoos that ordered them, then Larry's gift to me was his promise to give up capturing poisonous snakes."

The jungles were full of dazzling sights and sounds, but also contained a few surprises. Jungle Larry and Safari Jane had some close calls on safari. One time frightened Indian guides left Larry and Nancy to find their own way out of a jungle when they discovered the Tetzlaffs were there to hunt snakes. (One danger in the jungle is getting lost, because there are very few landmarks—nearly impenetrable trees and vines all over.)

Nancy told me, "While traveling through British Guyana in 1959, two headhunters jumped into our guide's jeep. Scared and unable to communicate, we pretended they weren't there. Five miles later, the natives jumped out at their destination. It turned out that these hitchhikers regularly rode with the Christian missionaries.

"In Liberia, West Africa, in 1966 our Land Rover's gas tank developed a hole. We were in the middle of nowhere. We couldn't afford to lose gas, so our guide fixed it with a wedge of pineapple. It got us back. Another time I woke up to a ten-inch tarantula on the mosquito netting covering my face."

The 1960 Safari

The Tetzlaffs presented film and animals to the Toledo Zoo, showing the rich game they encountered on their 1959 British Guyana and Brazil safari. The zoo trustees came up with the idea to have Larry take top executives of the zoo and *Toledo Blade* on safari and convinced the newspaper to underwrite the trip.

The Toledo Blade would not allow Nancy Jane to go on the trip because it was an all-male party. It was quite a blow to Nancy Jane to be left behind, but the money was good and Larry felt he had to go—even if it meant being without his usual safari partner.

In March of 1960, Larry departed with Toledo journalist Lew Klewer, Toledo Zoo Director Phil Skeldon, and the zoo's head curator, Dan Danford. Calling themselves "the Noah's Ark of the Air," they covered 20,000 miles by airplane, jeep, dugout canoe, horseback, and on foot. Work was done on a preliminary exploration Larry made with Safari Jane the year before. With $40,000, good luck, three hundred Indians and officials of South America, the safari was a success. Larry's DC 3 charter out of Georgetown, British Guyana, brought a record number of animals through Miami customs.

The paper reported that, while on safari, the group of four men particularly enjoyed the beauty of the Amazon and Brazil at dusk and dawn, when hundreds of bird songs were heard. They saw the rain forest's Kieteur Falls 741-foot drop—more than four times the height of Niagara Falls. Nancy said, "Larry and Lew Klewer put the Explorer's Club flag at the headwaters of the Amazon, where it flows from Guyana. Few travelers had ever been there aside from the natives."

A subsequent article said, "The dangers of the jungle are many. The brush hides jaguars. A careless kick at a rotten log may disclose a bushmaster, one of the world's deadliest reptiles, with fangs two inches long. While catching an arapaima, the world's largest species of freshwater fish that reaches a length of ten feet and a weight of 400 pounds, Larry was attacked by a caiman (a reptile similar to a crocodile and just as vicious), which he wrestled to subdue. After the trip Larry jested, 'The biggest thrill is getting out alive.' "

After fighting with two giant caiman Larry wrote one of many letters to Nancy about the latest catches and how he missed her. He described his visit with an Indian family whose beds were hammocks covered with cow hides for blankets. Larry had seen terrible fires everywhere, and even put one out. He had captured so many animals—anteaters, tortoises, and orioles in nests—that it took half the day, every day, to feed the babies, Larry told Nancy.

6.9 Larry on safari, with the arapaima he caught.

Coordinating a safari is exciting but detailed work. Weeks before leaving, the Tetzlaffs would notify the airline of approximately how many animals they planned to bring back. Through a guide, Larry had tribesmen standing by in the foreign country to flush the animals out into the open for Larry to catch in exchange for a little money or some trade-goods.

Once the animals were caught, Larry was responsible for hand-feeding his charges. He brought the basic food with him for his safari group and all the animals they might conceivably capture. Once the capturing began, Larry would get up before dawn to feed the animals already caught. Larry would then hunt all day, and if Nancy was on the trip, she would take pictures. Larry brought the new animals to camp where he fed them. The Tetzlaffs believe that animals have a right to humane treatment in captivity (even when captured on safari), including good food, veterinary care, and comfortable housing.

The birds and animals brought back by the 1960 *Toledo Blade* Zoo Safari were to be quarantined in San Juan, Puerto Rico. But the curasow birds had a fatal run-in with the British Guyana government. Nancy explained, "After Larry left Guyana, that government started a new regulation that birds be checked for yet another disease. At the time the vet examined the birds, he did not check for that particular disease, so he could not say the birds were free of it. Larry pleaded to be allowed to pay for those birds to be returned by airplane to Guyana. But the government gassed those birds. Larry was furious. Why should innocent birds die because somebody didn't check for a disease? It's things like that that gall you. In spite of this, in transit only a handful (a tenth of one percent) of birds died."

When capturing animals in the wild, Larry was well aware of conserving the breed. The natives were awed that Larry respected the birds. Nancy recalled, "Larry's philosophy was 'We'll take only six selected nests.' The locals didn't understand this. They said other collectors usually just came and cleaned them out! Larry took birds from their nests before they were old enough to fly so it was easier for them to adjust to captivity. He trapped birds at night, going up in the trees and shining lights on the birds after natives had baited them with a concoction that made the birds slightly drunk. Also, to get coconuts for that mixture, natives used to cut down the coconut palm trees. Larry taught them to pick the coconuts instead so the trees could continue to produce."

The safari group returned April 16, 1960, bringing one thousand animals of one hundred species with them. The safari netted forty different types of birds, including some new to the National Audubon Society. The safari party was greeted by hundreds of cheering well-wishers along the route from the Toledo airport to the zoo. Twelve thousand jammed the zoo for the welcome home program, according to reports in the paper.

The *Toledo Blade* Zoo Safari to British Guyana/Brazil legally brought back a 250-pound manatee, an arapaima fish, three rattlesnakes, anaconda constrictors, boas, many other unusual snakes, mata-mata turtles, anteaters, antbears, three three-toed sloths, spotted agoutis, a two-toed sloth, a variety of toads and frogs, monkeys (including sakis), a howler, capuchins, coatis, an ocelot, about two hundred tropical fish, two swinton kites, and other exotic birds, including burrowing owls, tanagers, curasows, a mot-mot bird, macaws, and five all-blue hyacinthian macaws, one of the rarest in American zoos, an article reported.

The Show Does Not Have to Go On

Working with animals can have its tense moments. Nancy said that "Larry realized he'd made a mistake one day in 1963, going in with a lioness when he had seen signs that she didn't want to work—just from the way she looked at him. He went in and Princess threw her ears down, squinted her eyes, and buried her claws in his shoulder. After that incident, he decided he could always drop one act and proceed to the next one."

6.10 Larry demonstrating how the movies make it look like the actors are being attacked and fighting with wild animals.

For an animal, the show doesn't always have to go on. If a performing animal doesn't want to have close contact on a given day, it's better to give the animal the day off than to risk having the trainer get injured. The Tetzlaffs, however, felt they must give their best in any case. If Larry was injured during a performance he usually managed to finish the show before taking care of his injury. Mike Cecere, related one such time. "On the second day I was [at work], I was helping Jungle Larry give an exhibit with snakes and an alligator when the young gator accidentally bit a piece of Larry's thumb off! Never missing a beat, Larry smiled, told a couple of jokes and excused himself. Nancy retrieved the end of Larry's thumb and took it and him for medical help. Meanwhile, Ralph and Ken Williams [Grounds Department] and I were left to round up the critters. While doing this a woman in the front row asked, 'Is that all there is of the show?' For Larry's amusement, Ralph later posted a sign on the alligator wrestling mat Jungle Larry used: Alligators—1; Alligator Wrestlers—0."

For awhile, Larry also wrestled with a jaguar in his act, but after one too many close calls gave it up. One day the jaguar decided not to let Jungle Larry go, holding him by the ear. It took a long time, but Larry finally talked the animal into releasing him.

In all, Larry was clawed by a leopard, a jaguar, and lions, bitten by poisonous snakes, thrown by an elephant, and kicked  by a zebra. Throughout thousands of performances and many years of training and handling animals and snakes, Larry had only a few injuries that caused him to miss shows. His policy of putting safety first resulted in a commendable record.

7

Jungle Larry's Legacy

We had two dogs, Fritz, a miniature Schnauzer, and Gizmo, a standard poodle. When we brought a new cub home, whether a lion, tiger, or tiglon [a tiger-lion mix], the dogs were bigger and they bossed the cats around, thinking they're hot stuff. As the wild cats grew, gradually the dogs were looking at eye level at the big cat, then looking up to him, then looking further up to him. Usually the dog totally backed away like, 'Okay, you're bigger than I am,' but sometimes the dog maintained that dominant role—if that big cat could be bossed. —Tim Tetzlaff

IN 1962, five years after Jungle Larry and Safari Jane were married, their first child, David Lawrence, was born. He was given Lawrence as a middle name in case he ever wanted to carry on the Jungle Larry name. When Tim arrived in 1968, the family also gave him the Lawrence option as part of his name. Years later, though, Larry said he was proud that David wanted to be known by his own name rather than ride on his dad's coattails as the next "Jungle Larry."

David's first TV appearance was on Thanksgiving 1962 when he was six weeks old. The show required no rehearsal for him; he just touched a huge python.

Larry was a devoted father despite his fame. Nancy told me, "He was a very good-looking man, with a very distinctive voice. Despite the safari, gator-wrestling life-style, Larry didn't show his years.

"People would request pictures of Larry with the family. I can't tell you how many dear children he held in their dirty, leaking, wet diapers. Thinking, 'Oh, another one,' he never said anything to the people. Afterward, he'd just wash. We enjoyed the public; we did not mind talking to the people or signing autographs. The people are what kept us alive and made us popular on TV. They are important and if they're not coming any more, then you've lost it."

As pre-school-age children, before the Tetzlaff boys saw their dad with the public or on TV, they weren't impressed with their father's work. Like kids in other families, they thought of their father only as dad. Nancy said, "When they recognized their father as Jungle Larry on TV, they seemed astonished, 'That's you, isn't it, Dad?'"

At home, Larry was not the showman, but a conscientious parent. Despite all the time constraints, Larry made time to be there for the children's births, to bathe and feed them, baby-sit and to change diapers.

At the Naples park, David talked to me about his father. Drawing his long legs into the golf cart, we rode to the meat house to get the leopard's lunch that was prepared earlier that morning.

"When I was in grade school, we'd go to dinner and movies just like other families. My dad liked going to the beach or the circus. So I really haven't changed much," he chuckled. "I do that same old stuff. But sometimes Dad would have weekends off and we'd like to work out in the yard and be regular people. So if he was trimming trees in the yard, I had to pick up branches before I could ride my skateboard. So that's where I got this thing of work first, then you play. So today I get everything cleaned, the meat cut, then I've got my head clear to practice with the tigers."

The family also took vacations together. David said, "I'm glad I went a lot of places when I was younger, because I don't have the time now. We went up to Canada a couple of times, Mexico twice, Grand Cayman, Caribbean, and out West to a dude ranch in Arizona. My dad made time for us. I'm talking about later in his career, when he was in his fifties. When he was my age he was doing everything: cleaning, feeding, and performing, like I am now."

I asked Tim about his perspective of his father's fame. We sat on a concrete bench near the park's Lake Victoria. "My dad is more of a hero to me the more I find out about him. I'm still finding out stuff. That large marble memorial here at the park

The Tetzlaff family portrait that was used for their 1969 Christmas card.

David completes the difficult six-tiger lay down with the Bengal tigers.

David (right) has made a number of trips to Europe to meet with notable animal trainers and circus people. Here he is shown (left to right) with David Jamieson, Jim Clubb, and Gerd Seimoniet.

David and Centaine doing the pirouette sequence.

Nancy Jane, Art Kozlik, and a wolf welcome one of the many media personalities to visit the park at Cedar Point.

David becomes part of the Indian leopard blanket.

David and Shikar take a break before the gates open at Cedar Point.

A proud mother on Mother's Day with her two sons.

David training an Indian leopard cub and a young African elephant to accept one another.

Jungle Larry with his lion act at Cedar Point.

133

Safari Jane tells Amber a secret.

Tim and his wife, Kathryn, joining the family at holiday times.

Nancy and Bob enjoying a Caribbean cruise in 1988.

Java completing a difficult leap through an extra-small, fifteen-inch hoop.

David and a black leopard cub take time out on the couch after a busy day.

David and Tim train a young tiger during exercise time to walk on a leash.

Visitors may read the impressive memorial plaque to Jungle Larry at the Naples Park.

David and Ralph Williams preparing to load the animals in the truck for the annual trek from Florida to Ohio.

David with Tina, the African lioness that he raised from a cub.

The Safari kid.

David (right) introducing the golden tabby tiger to Jack Hanna, director emeritus of the Columbus Zoo.

Just before they leave for the Moscow Circus, Russian trainers Olga and Sarwat Begbudi and their white tigers that were quarantined at Cedar Point, enjoy a last visit with David and Mindy.

David, age twenty, presenting one of the African Safari trained elephants.

Nancy Jane with a young captive-bred chimpanzee.

Sasha, David and Mindy's son, at age four, summer 1992.

Nancy Jane with the lion cub that was to become a star performer in both the Ohio and Florida shows.

David as a teen-ager, skateboarding—his favorite pastime when not training to be a trainer.

Nancy Jane Tetzlaff-Berens, 1994.

Bob Berens and David (left) with one of the white tigers which was sold to the Moscow Circus.

Sasha and Mindy.

David catching the Indian leopard, Honey, as she leaps into his arms.

Larry with sons David and Tim.

pared Dad's list of accomplishments at least in half. Dad didn't brag about his past to us at home. Consequently, I learned more about his achievements at our employee appreciation dinners that were held at the house or a restaurant. During those he'd tell stories about his amazing past. My dad was of the temperament that if a zoo had asked him for an alligator and if this lake had any, and one swam by, my dad would jump in fully clothed, just to get it."

Cubs in the House

David and Tim grew up at the Ohio and Florida parks as much as in their home. Conversely, many newly-born cat cubs, chimps, reptiles and various birds, including ostrich chicks, spent their early months in the Tetzlaff house, before moving to the park. Brutus and Duchess, both lion cubs, had the run of the house in 1966. People joke about kid-proofing a house to protect valuables and breakables from their toddlers. Put up the glass trinkets from the coffee table, move the silk throws, and so on. But how do you lion-proof a house? Remove the couch and chairs?

Tim said one of his earliest memories was in 1969 when he was a toddler. He recalls that the newborn tiglons had a lot of fun chewing on couch pillows and suede jackets. The Tetzlaffs had several couches ruined by cubs playing with the cushions. They accepted the damage as part of hand-raising playful wild animals.

Tim reminisced about spending his entire childhood with various litters of two or three cubs. "We raised a lot of leopard pairs. I remember helping care for Missy, one of David's black leopards. At the Sandusky house we had a couch that stretched out in front of the TV—one of these sectional couches you could make into any shape. It was made almost into a bed, so you could lay there and watch TV. The leopard would be 'tooling' around the house, jump over the back of the couch, and just land right on whoever was on the couch. After a while I'd put a pillow on me so she'd jump on that instead of me."

While David's friends played, David preferred to rush home from school to help feed the leopards and lions. Cubs were fed formula from a baby bottle every four to six hours, until they were old enough for the Tetzlaffs to introduce a mixture of fresh ground meat, condensed milk, water, and vitamins.

Besides feeding the cubs, the Tetzlaffs also had to massage the cubs' rear ends to simulate a mother's licking. This was done to promote bowel movements, so the cubs wouldn't get constipated and possibly die. Tim said, "When I was about thirteen years old, I remember taking young cubs to our chain link fenced back yard, bringing a wet paper towel to simulate the mother cat's tongue. I'd hold up the tail of the animal and rub its behind a little bit to stimulate it to go to the bathroom. It's neat when it works. You have to be patient. Then it would hunker down, and I thought 'YES—now I can go inside as soon as she finishes!' "

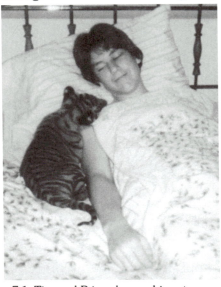

7.1 Tim and Prince have a big cat nap.

Tim continued, "Prince is another cub we raised. He now weighs about five hundred pounds and is the second-biggest tiger in David's show. I have pictures of him as a cub lying in bed next to me, and a picture of us playing on the couch. I also have pictures of that cub face to face with our white ten-pound domestic cat."

The Tetzlaffs offered cubs a smooth transition from being hand raised in the house to living with their peers in the park. Nancy told me, "During the day the litter of two or three would take the ten-minute car trip to the park with us. For the day they were out in a playpen [8' x 8' x 4'] that was placed upside down, so it had a roof instead of a floor. They had their toys in there. We had it outside the office area so they could get used to the people and the park noises. As they got older, we walked the cubs on leashes. When it was time for them to be at the park full-time, they would have their own area. We still gave them attention, so they had a nice transition from the different homes. We'd never have an animal go cold turkey from a home to the park."

When David and the cats were young, his peers often wanted to see his "pets." He felt it was no big deal when his friends wanted to come over to see the cubs at his house. "I guess I took it for granted. 'Yeah, I got a lion cub,' " he said without bragging. "I never used this place to make friends. I just accepted it as part of my life and didn't feel used by it. Nor did I want to give the animals the feeling of being used."

7.2 Blanco, the family cat, and Prince (right).

Hi Ho Days and Childhood Fun

Because the park was open every day of the year, when David was young his parents compensated for the family's missed holidays by creating Hi Ho days: they would take a day off and leave the work to the park employees. Nancy explained, "With children, Christmas and birthday are the two highlights of the year. Instead of celebrating one birthday, throughout the year we made our own holidays as we could—our Hi Ho days. We started this tradition when we had only David. 'Okay, today is Hi Ho day!' He knew that was his day. We'd go to the store and buy something David really liked and ask him where he wanted to go, and what he wanted to do and see."

When David and Tim (nicknamed "Tiger") were in elementary school, their closest friends in Ohio were Paul Pifer and John Illig, who were a year or two older than David. But David says he was the ringleader, always coming up with ideas of where to go and what to do. Paul's mother, Billie Pifer, still lives in Sandusky in the same house on the block where these four boys spent their summers. Mrs. Pifer told me, "For a period of time they would go over on the beach to get quartz from the rocks." She laughed. "They spent hours over at the rocks with their hammers and screwdrivers to come home with a little handful of quartz. They had a period of time it was GI Joes and over on the beach they'd go and do an army routine. Then everybody was skateboarding, and Nancy would take them to a park with skateboard ramps."

7.3 Merry Christmas from the Tetzlaff boys, 1975.

When I talked to Paul, he told me about growing up with the Tetzlaffs as friends. "When I was eight years old we moved to Sandusky from a Cleveland suburb. The Tetzlaffs lived two houses down. My father was a bigwig at Cedar Point and was Jungle Larry's immediate supervisor. It was easy for us boys to become close friends.

"We only spent summers together. It's really strange when you see a close friend only four months each year. We'd hear from the Tetzlaffs once or twice during the winter; when they'd come back in late May we'd all aged and matured a year.

"Every summer was fun. I'd look forward to when Dave and Tim would come. I'd go over to the house and the safari park and romp and play and take road trips with the whole family. We'd all pile in their van, David, John, me and Tim, and go to skateboard parks, the malls, Cleveland, to amusement parks or Sea

7.4 Young David practices
his Tarzan yell.

World. The summers with the Tetzlaffs were incredible."

Paul laughed throughout his warm reminiscence. "And of course, when you travel with Jungle Larry, you go sit down in a restaurant in Sandusky and fifteen people get up and come over to ask for his autograph. It started out being kind of fun then I got to where I just kind of looked the other way thinking, 'Oh, not again.' Most of the fun stuff I did between eight to thirteen years of age was with the Tetzlaffs, my second family. It was just a darn good time. A really good way to grow up."

7.5 "Tiger" Tim and a lion cub take a break from play.

During the summer of 1972, when David was ten, he and a few neighborhood friends wanted to raise money for World Wildlife Fund. So they organized a circus in the Tetzlaff's backyard.

Nancy recalled, "The kids putting on the show dressed up in outfits like lion trainers and clowns. Our fenced back yard was the performing area and the audience had to be on the outside of the fence. One of our trainers came over from the park with a couple of animals—whatever ones David or Tim could handle. We'd have a young chimp, a cub, a bird, any of the small animals or snakes. Kids and their moms thought it was great. In one summer's show the boys raised close to one hundred dollars in twenty-five cent admissions." The circus was repeated the following summer.

Paul clearly remembers these fund raisers. "My all-time favorite thing is the cowboys-and-Indians play we put on during one of these carnivals. Five- or six-year-old Tim was an Indian, running along, getting shot and still running. His mother yelled at him, 'Tim! You're shot! Lay down!' and he looked over at her and at the crowd and he yelled, 'But Mom, Indians don't die!' and kept running. We like to remind him of that from time to time. 'Indians don't die.' "

As he grew up, David was responsible and sensitive. By the time he was thirteen, he wanted expensive shirts and tennis shoes. His parents told him they would give him the money for an average pair of tennis shoes. If he wanted to pay extra for designer shoes, he could earn it. So he did, earning money by mowing neighbors' yards. One Sandusky neighbor, Mrs. Helms, reflected on David's consideration. "When I went to pay him, one time he noticed it was the last five-dollar bill in my purse and he said, 'Am I going to run you short?' and I thought for a youngster his age, about thirteen or fourteen, he was so considerate. I smiled and told him he wouldn't run me short."

1972 Photography Safari

Besides organizing animal-capturing safaris for zoos, Larry enjoyed escorting small groups on sightseeing and photography safaris. Up to fifteen travelers at a time went with Jungle Larry to see and photograph wild animals in their natural habitat. The trips were very educational. Larry concentrated on showing the difficulties faced by many species.

Nancy explained, "For one thing, the veldt or jungle was not overloaded with animals—and the group would search to find the animals. In the wild state you also see animals that are deprived of adequate food supply and veterinary care—not as perfect specimens as in captivity. You get a realistic view of how tough it is to live in the wild where only the fittest survive."

Whether in captivity or in the wild, to see magnificent animals is stunning. Nancy continued, "When you see the animals in the wild you see the balance of how the native out in the bush is fighting to have space to raise food for his family. He is subject to a troop of baboons, antelope, or elephants cleaning him out. You see the battle that the native African has in surviving and you see the battle the animal has in surviving."

David went with his parents on safaris when he was so little he no longer remembers them—to West Africa when he was three and one-half years old and to the Yucatan when he was four and one-half. But when David was nine years old, he went with his dad and a sightseeing group to East Africa. Nancy elaborated, "That 1972 safari covered Kenya, Tanzania (where in Manyara National Park, lions actually climb trees and lie up in the limbs), and Uganda. In fact, theirs was one of the last groups in and out of Uganda when Idi Amin ruled. Larry said when they went in the Entebbe airport some of the people had their cameras out and they were warned to not film anything. A few weeks later Uganda was shut down completely."

7.6 David makes friends with a spot-nosed monkey in Liberia in 1966.

David remembers that safari vividly. "People think of Africa as very hot, but it's actually cool where the lush growth reaches so high the sun doesn't come through. . . . " He paused. "Three weeks—just me and Dad. It was neat because my dad was boss and everybody looked to him for everything. In the hills going from Kenya to Tanzania, it'd been raining and raining, and the bus got stuck. The drivers were out with machetes, cutting sticks and branches to stick under the wheels. My dad was right out there with these men he'd hired for transportation. I was impressed that wild lions, not zoo lions, could have come up behind the men working to loose the vehicle."

In Africa, however, you can drive a jeep as close as you want to many animals. Lions become accustomed to the numerous buses crowding around daily. The lions were undisturbed by the vehicles because they weren't shot at. David remarked, "Cheetahs get kind of used to having vehicles around, too. But leopards don't want any part of it. We saw two leopards when we were there and we were lucky. A lot of people who have been there have never seen one."

7.7 When David was in East Africa in 1972, he met a warrior from the Mt. Kenya Safari club.

Eileen Hofmaster, a long-time family friend, recalled that 1972 safari. "It's been twenty years. I haven't forgotten it. At the Ark in the Aberdere Forest is a lodge built near a large waterhole. From the verandahs you can see a specially-built salt lick. A dungeon room allows people to go down and stare at elephants at eye level with a six-foot wall between. The waterhole is lit up at night and employees watch from their verandahs and ring a bell when they see an animal at the watering hole. They rang that bell a lot and I was always there first. I saw thirty-two elephants in one-half hour. Other animals that came to the water hole were cape buffalo, leopard, rhino, hyena, white-tailed mongoose, exotic birds and a little rabbit."

In the Serengeti Game Reserve, the sightseers also saw giraffes, zebras, a variety of antelope family such as wildebeests, hartebeests, elands, impalas, waterbucks, and gazelles. During the trip they also saw a few cheetahs, hippos, baboons, and colobus monkeys. The safari group collectively photographed hundreds of rolls of pictures of wild animals and scenery.

After School at Jungle Larry's

From the time David could push a broom, he helped his folks out at the family business. Until his third year in high school, David was a model student. While cutting meat for the cats, David confided, "I was a senior at Naples High School when I started training my leopards, and the next morning I went to school and looked at everything like 'What am I doing here? This is so immature. This is not important to me any more.' Once you start working with animals, you're different. It was like stepping into the real world from the classroom. It was good that in my senior year I had enough credits so I only had to take two classes. I was out of school by 10:00 A.M. and over here working."

Despite his lack of enthusiasm for school, David graduated in 1981, ranking twenty-seventh out of a class of 240 students. But he didn't want to go to college; he couldn't leave the animals. "It's addicting. It's such a joy working with animals, putting together an act. And if it's something that the crowd enjoys, that's super."

David, Tim, Paul, and John remained a tight boyhood group. When they were old enough to have part-time jobs, each boy chose to work at Ohio's Jungle Larry's: David and Tim doing a little bit of everything with the animals; Paul as a trail guide, before Larry made him a snake curator. Later, John trained animals for the park under David's supervision.

All four boys decided on careers with animals. Paul is a successful veterinarian in Ohio. John now works for Jim Clubb, an animal trainer in England and has presented a polar, Himalayan, and grizzly bear act that the Circus Friends Association of Great Britain (CFA) Circus Awards voted Best Animal Act in 1991.

Tim

Tim was every bit as active in the life of the park when he was growing up as David was. When he was just three years old, Tim did reptile lectures, and later, at age eleven, had a magician's booth at Cedar Point Safari where he did magic tricks for the guests between Jungle Larry's shows. For several years, before he was old enough to clean and feed the animals, he loved magic. Nancy said when she asked him how he had accomplished a particular trick, Tim would answer with a smile, "Very well, since I fooled you, Mom."

During their first eighteen years, David and Tim shared the same experiences. David began performing with trained elephants and chimps while Tim began with a pony act. "We hired Mike Rice, a well-known elephant and horse trainer to teach Tim to learn how to train horses," Nancy said. "Each day after school, he would come to the park and practice with Mike. This act became very polished and in 1982, at age fourteen, he presented it at Cedar Point. It was very well received. He was 'cool' in the arena when one day a pony stepped on the back of his shoe and it partially came off. Tim calmly stepped out of the shoe and finished the show with one shoe on and one shoe off. I still laugh when I think about it. He never missed a step or cue," said Nancy.

He spent his summers working at the Cedar Point Safari in one job or another, including ranger and lecturer, until at age twelve, he learned to prepare animal diets in the commissary. Then, when Tim was fifteen, he learned how to be David's back-up—a major responsibility which he did well.

Nancy says,"Tim's gentle ways and his love of the classics, writing and communication skills led him into teaching high school English literature after his graduation from Ohio State. He will benefit many students due to his background, his Christian foundation and activity in church and his desire to impart knowledge."

After his marriage to Kathryn Belgen, Tim and his wife lived for awhile at the Naples park in a guest cottage. He vividly described what it is like to live with big cats—to arrive at the park at dawn. "About 5:00 in the morning you'd hear the lions start roaring. It's amazing. When I was working in the cat department, my wife and I would come out on the lake in the morning—in spring it's warm out early. I'd let all the cats out of their buildings in their yards before the sun came up. Usually about sunrise I'd be coming down the path, and a lot of times the fog would just be lifting off this lake and you've got the sun rising over there—

just extraordinary. With the impinging concrete jungle outside, you wonder how this paradise still remains," he said.

7.8 Tim and David, 1988.

Tim and Kathryn, an alumna of Columbus College of Art and Design, hope to work in Central or South America someday. They have surrounded themselves with cats in their home in Columbus, Ohio—not exotic cats but five of the domestic variety. As Nancy says, "Tim needs to have animals in his daily life." Even when Tim is away, he still has emotional ties to the animals and park and looks forward to holiday visits in Naples.

Both sons provided invaluable help to Nancy in the years following Larry's death, helping her successfully take over operations of the park. "Larry would be proud of both our sons," said Nancy. And she is proud that her two sons are carrying on the traditions of their famous father—animal training and education.

A Tradition of Conservation

"Jungle Larry was a conservationist long before being one was popular," Nancy said. "He loved to educate people about conservation, informing them that trees hold moisture in the soil and that trees cool the surroundings. Larry was disappointed that man continued to tear up huge trees for real-estate development. He wanted to save the earth's pure water, vegetation, and animals. He often talked about the future of wild animals. In 1972, he told park visitors that in the previous year eighty-nine species of fish, birds, and mammals had become extinct and fifteen more species were now endangered," she said.

Nancy told me that many species must now be bred in captivity to survive. Larry always hoped his animals would reproduce not only so he could sell the offspring to other zoos but keep the species going. Today it's hard to believe alligators were nearly extinct in the late 1960s. Larry had a big part in their preservation. In 1968 in the Everglades National Park, the last stronghold of the alligator, the reptile was endangered because poachers nightly killed gators for their hides. The park was simply too large for its staff to patrol. Hides were smuggled out of the United States to Europe, made into shoes, purses, and belts, and then brought back to be sold in American stores. As a result of Jungle Larry's film *Vanishing Everglades*, which was shown in schools, hundreds of children wrote letters to the Department of the Interior to try to 'Save our Everglades!' More rangers were hired and heavy fines were imposed on violators. The program was successful. Today the alligator is thriving in Florida.

Many times Larry was asked whether his animals could survive out in the wild. He answered that they could because they are wild animals, not domesticated ones. Even those born in captivity show their wildness eight generations later, he said.

Living near the edge of the Everglades, Larry had a soft spot for the animals that lived there. He put food out for wild animals when they had difficulty surviving, such as during the drought of 1980. In that drought, hundreds of animals came to the park's edge for food and water.

Nancy elaborated, "Larry also put out food when there were fires in the Everglades. We'd go out to the driveway to get the morning newspaper and smell the smoke even here in the city. We felt for the people who lived out there. We set out extra food in the wild, dense areas of the property to help animals survive without coming too close to the park."

Resident Cats

In the 1970s, the Tetzlaffs had more than sixty tigers, lions, leopards, jaguars, and tiglons on exhibit and in shows. Jungle Larry especially enjoyed the cats, saying they were some of the most responsive animals to work with.

Nancy talked fondly of the regular park walks that she and Larry would take to greet their feline family. This was how the

Tetzlaffs liked to unwind and enjoy their animal family and each other. During those walks Larry and Nancy often imitated the call of the big cats, who usually would answer.

Many of the park's animals were named by the public through contests—the Tetzlaffs' way of encouraging customers' participation in the park. Larry and Nancy took cubs on TV and asked people to mail in name entries. Then, as a family, they would pick the winning names from among the hundreds of entries. The last contest, Nancy recalled, was to name her four tigers, Kahn, Sinbad, Misha, and Jasmine. Jungle Larry's no longer holds contests to name animals, primarily because David likes to name his own animals.

Breeding Tiglons and Dreaming Supercats

Tigers are normally found in Asia, and lions in Africa, so the species never meet. If the two species were to become friendly, conception would still be unlikely, because their chromosome balance is different. Despite the genetic difficulties, animal breeders have long been interested in crossbreeding a lioness with a tiger to create a "tiglon."

7.9 Jungle Larry with the parents of the tiglons.

The tiglons' offspring end up with characteristics of both breeds—the stripes of a tiger and the tawny color of lions. Tiglons have personality traits from both parents, perhaps acting like a reclusive tiger one day and a socialite lion the next. Larry and Nancy's most famous breeding experiment was to crossbreed a tiger with a lion.

Another combination of breeding using male lions and female tigers produces "ligers." More ligers have been born than tiglons, since lions are more social than male tigers.

The Tetzlaffs weren't the only tiglon breeders. Ten years earlier Evelyn Curie, a descendant of French scientists Pierre and Marie Curie, was presenting a lion and tiger act in the Ringling Circus when an accidental breeding produced a single female tiglon. Another female was born to Hollywood actress Tippi Hedren's lioness. (Hedren has a compound to save wild animals in California.) But the Tetzlaffs had the first triplets, two of which were the first male tiglons, Rajah and Sultan, and Maharani, a female.

Larry had tried to crossbreed lions with tigers for seventeen years even though everybody told him he was wasting his time. But the lions and tigers routinely worked together in Larry's harmony acts. Because Rajah the tiger got along with Princess, the lioness, Larry started supervising these two animals first ten, then fifteen, then twenty minutes a day, until finally the tiger and lion were living together twenty-four hours a day. But when Princess came in season, the pair wouldn't mate. Larry realized this was because the animals weren't hearing the customary species' mating calls. So Larry and the staff imitated the tiger's "pfft" and lion's "ooom." Each animal apparently thought the other had made the receptive mating sound and the plan worked.

In May of 1969, the tiglons were conceived and triplets were born at Cedar Point on September 21. Larry filmed them at five days old for the NBC "Today Show." When the cubs were three weeks old they were flown in the first-class section to Florida to be hand-raised.

The Tetzlaffs felt the tiglons showed more love to humans than any other breed they had trained in thirty years. The tiglons were affectionate, gentle, intelligent animals, willing to learn their tricks at ten months of age. Larry's act consisted of the tiglons sitting up, jumping through a hoop, walking a tightrope, and wrestling with Larry.

Although the tiglons enjoyed long lives at the park and even mated, they were unable to reproduce. The Tetzlaffs unsuccessfully tried mating a tiglon with a tiger, then with a lioness. The

Tetzlaffs thought if the animals would breed naturally, fine. As with all their animals, they did not want to use artificial means to force the tiglons to reproduce.

Jungle Larry's dream was to breed jaguars, leopards, tigers, lions, and tiglons to produce a supercat. They'd breed tiglons to leopards or jaguars and then these offspring with each other. He foresaw a huge animal with the tiger's bulk, the jag's great strength, the leopard's speed and cunning, the lion's beautiful great mane. Tiguars, leolions, jagards, and ligers. Larry felt cross-breeds were extremely intelligent. He estimated it would take ten years to complete all the breeding, because of the rarity of the breeding. But this dream was one of the few Larry was unable to fulfill, Nancy told me.

Honors

Besides the rewards of working with Frank Buck, Captain Penny, and Johnny Weismuller, Larry was the recipient of many formal honors. He served as a field editor of *Safari* magazine for several years. In the 1960s, after following Larry around for a week, *Look* magazine editors said that he was probably the most popular adult in Ohio. And, Larry was appointed honorary Kentucky Colonel for his work in conservation.

7.10 Captain Penny and Jungle Larry examine the story in *Look* magazine that called Larry the most popular man in Ohio. (courtesy of WEWS)

Acknowledged as an animal expert, Larry was one of a team of experts appointed in 1970 by the governor of Florida to determine minimum cage standards for zoo animals. In the 1930s through the 1950s, many poorly kept roadside exhibits detracted from Florida's efforts to create a new image. Some of these substandard exhibits were even licensed. Tourists wrote to the state saying they had a great time in Florida except for the pitiful wild animal shows along the road that stuck in their minds. Animals had inadequate water supplies, cages were dirty, and there were no shelters from sun or rain. Some attractions had unclean wooden floors with soaked up urine and excrement. Some places didn't have guardrails and children had been bitten by monkeys.

This task force worked nonstop for two days and nights on the recommendations that became law July 1, 1972. Enforced by the Fish and Game Commission, the law remains much the same today. Most other states adopted those minimum cage standards. The law contained no provisions for fines or jail terms but allows the Commission to confiscate any animals and thereby save the animals from inhumane treatment even if it means putting someone out of business.

In 1972 and 1973 Larry served as president of the Florida Attractions Association, an organization established to uphold agreed-upon standards of family-oriented entertainment for Florida tourists.

Undoubtedly, Larry's top honor was being inducted into the Explorers' Club in 1983. The club's distinguished members include explorers and scientists who have contributed to finding new frontiers or expanding the world's knowledge, such as Admiral Byrd, Commander Robert Perry, Lowell Thomas, John Glenn, Neil Armstrong, Sir Edmund Hilary, Charles Lindbergh, Marlin Perkins, and Jim Fowler.

The Park's Influence on Careers

"I can't tell you how many workers spent a summer with us then chose a career with animals. Many former staff and employees keep in touch," said Nancy as she told me of one example. "In the 1960s I hired Donna, the first girl who worked for us. In fact, she was going to be a nurse until working here. That summer changed her whole life. She now has a Ph.D in animal behavior, has been to Africa, and has gotten grants to study the thirteen-lined squirrel in Utah, where she went to school."

Trainers who are now all over the world got their training from Jungle Larry, Safari Jane, or David. Wade Burck, a well-known tiger trainer at Ringling's, started at Jungle Larry's. Mike Cecere was a young trainer when he joined Jungle Larry's. He changed his "gladiator" style of circus training for the European methods used by Larry. He now manages the Double M Ranch Historical American Circus in Hastings, New York.

When Roy Wells was nineteen, he came to the park as a trail guide. He began training chimps and elephants with Larry and went on to become the head trainer when he was twenty-five years old. He trained a variety of animals, but his specialties were tiger acts and elephant acts. Wells travels as an independent elephant trainer and handler contracting with various circuses.

Wells helped train Pat White, who in 1977, at twenty-one years of age was possibly the youngest woman to present wild animals in the country. While she was at Jungle Larry's, Pat worked under the direction of Wells, learning how to train and present the chimps and lions that Wells had trained. She has traveled throughout Canada and the United States with various circuses and currently works lions for the Yano circus in Japan. For a time she retired from the arena to create magnificent art in cast bronze— one of them called "Celestial Circus," with seven circus animals spiraling out of the circus top.

7.11 Roy Wells successfully trained an elephant, a lion, and a chimp to perform together.

What Prominent Trainers Say

Pat White spoke of the animal care and safety being the main thing she learned from the Tetzlaffs. "The lessons I learned during the three years I worked for Larry and Nancy I carried with me throughout my entire career—health, nutrition, cleanliness, safety were all things of utmost importance. There was never to be anything in the cage with the animal except dry sawdust, fresh water, and a toy or a bowling ball for a tiger."

7.12 Pat White performing her circus act.

Pat recalls: "When I was in college, I was hired as a guide—someone who strolled around the compound saying: 'On our left is an anteater, on our right is a tiglon.' A couple of months later I knew that I wanted to work the animals. What I wanted to do was cats, of course, but you just didn't walk in off the streets and start working cats. The route you went was first you worked the chimps, then the elephants, then you worked the cats. So I started at the beginning—weaseling my way into the chimp act in 1974, unbeknownst to Larry and Nancy. I started doing the 8:00 P.M. shows [under the supervision of Wells]. Of course, I got caught, but instead of firing me they hired me full time both in Florida and Ohio and I never went back to college. By 1975, I was living on the Naples park grounds and raising the four lion cubs that I began training for my act when they were about three months old."

Mike Cecere also spoke to me of the Tetzlaff's support. "[They] are two of the finest people I've ever been associated with. They would buy or build any type of prop I asked for and would back the training of any act, no matter how long it took to get it ready for public presentation."

Wells spoke of the standards at Jungle Larry's. "They were always willing to buy different animals for me to work with—whatever I wanted. And they always had a clean operation. Unlike some places where a mess accumulates, you never see any feces in the Jungle Larry's cages. It's a first-class operation."

Wells compared the three Tetzlaff trainers. "Larry was a good P.R. person. The animals seemed to work even better for Nancy than Larry. However, she didn't have as much of a chance to work with the animals, because Larry always had her busy running the office. But the animals seemed to respond for her. Larry was good with the animals, and with educating the people. But David is far superior to his father, handling the animals and talking to the people both."

Jungle Larry and Safari Jane Step Out of the Ring

In 1982, Jungle Larry retired from working in the cage and prepared David to succeed him. He kept busy for the next two years as proud director of the successful zoological park.

Nancy also stepped out of the arena in 1982. "I had worked with my four Bengal tigers but had to be away from them for a period of months. The tigers were two years old and had spent all their time at the Naples park. David was willing to work with them in Ohio, but I was very stubborn. 'No, David, don't work with them. When I get to Ohio I'll work with them. This is my act.' When I got up there the tigers were scared, because there were no leaves on the trees and they could see through their cages to the moving roller coaster. It probably looked like a monster to them. The tigers chased me out of the arena a couple of times. They gave Larry a hard time. They gave David a hard time. They

7.13 Jungle Larry and Safari Jane pose with handsome tiglon, circa 1982.

never would work at Cedar Point. It really verified that you have to take young animals into whatever situations they'll be working in."

Nancy candidly said she quit working the cats because she felt David's act had surpassed hers. "After I [had trouble with] the tigers and David was doing so beautifully with his leopards, I felt that we didn't need another act or trainer out there."

8

The End of an Era

Even toward the end, he was valuable to us just sitting out on the trail talking to people. He could tell you one story after another for hours and never stop talking about animals. —Art Kozlik, manager of the Cedar Point operation

WITHIN A YEAR of leaving the arena, while Jungle Larry was writing an article about rain forests and thoroughly enjoying his new role of managing the park, he died unexpectedly.

Nancy told me that it was hard at first to deal with the media. The family wanted privacy, but they were receiving calls from all over when word spread of Jungle Larry's death. "I knew how Larry felt about death. He didn't want a big to-do. He didn't want a big funeral service or anything. He had said, 'However I die, let people remember me like I was when they visited the park. Let them remember the Jungle Larry that they have in their hearts.' "

Weary, and trying to respect Larry's wishes, Nancy asked Channel 5 in Cleveland not to air a tribute. But the station noted that other television channels were already planning to do a big spread. A representative of Channel 5 begged Nancy for permission to use footage that the station had because of Larry's long relationship with the channel. Her mother told Nancy, who was in Naples at the time of the broadcast, that the program was beautiful and even Ted Henry, the anchorman, was choked up.

The unexpected death of the legendary Jungle Larry was difficult for the family. The family had a private service at home in the afternoon, Nancy explained, "and I was back to work the next day with my door shut. It was my way of surviving. I couldn't stay home and look at those walls."

Nancy confided, "I felt the closest to Larry here at the park. Everyone handles grief differently. The [park] was my comfort zone. I was very grateful when my Cedar Point boss, Bill Nelson, called and asked 'What do you want to do this summer? Do you want to come back?' Fervently I said, 'Yes, I want to come home!' He replied, 'I'm glad to hear that.' Of course, I knew that during that first summer I was in a fishbowl. I knew they were watching everything I did and making sure I was capable of running it. Over the years they saw Larry and me running it together."

The animals were also affected by Jungle Larry's sudden disappearance. Shortly after Larry's death, Nancy resumed the morning trail walks she and her husband had regularly taken.

Nancy continued with tears in her eyes, "One of the hardest things after Larry died—I'd go out after closing and walk the park for hours. I'd get the greetings from the animals and they'd look behind me for Larry. I couldn't explain to them that he wouldn't be coming back. They knew we belonged together. They'd love and greet me and then look down the trail. It was a long time before the cats gave up looking.

"I also sat with Tim's ponies a lot when I had to get away and be alone. They were a beautiful reddish color with blond manes. They came up when I'd be sitting there crying and put their little muzzles on me, just like they knew. Animals give their love unreservedly. If you're ever feeling really blue you can go sit with them and they make you feel A-okay."

The Public Mourns

Larry's work has also touched many other lives. When Nancy received a large number of sympathy cards and letters, she realized Larry's profound affect on others. People from all over the world wrote to tell her what beautiful memories they had of Larry's work and his family. "I collected a big box, a foot deep, of the most beautiful cards and letters from people I didn't even know."

The family had several ways to show their love for Larry. First, the Tetzlaffs erected a granite plaque at the Naples park in memory of the gentleman who affected three generations. The inscription:

In loving memory, Jungle Larry, Colonel Lawrence Tetzlaff, who always loved people and animals.

Outstanding showman, animal trainer, television star, author, lecturer, motion picture producer, herpetologist, double for Tarzan, expedition leader to Australia, South America, and Africa, developed the crossbreed of tiglons, conservationist, member of the Explorers' Club, former president of the Florida Attractions Association, and Governors' Wildlife Committee for Florida.

8.1 Col. Lawrence Tetzlaff, affectionately known as Jungle Larry.

The family also created the Jungle Larry Scholarship at Santa Fe Community College in Gainesville for the animal keeper training program. Nancy said the best way she could show her love for Larry was to continue his work as the family's living memorial.

Nancy said in retrospect, she would have taken more time off to simply have fun with Larry. "From personal experience, I say don't work yourself to death thinking when you reach a certain age you're going to quit and then enjoy life. After Larry died and I started putting my life back together, I decided I would take time to smell the roses. Don't wait to the end of the road. I may not have been able to change Larry's dying, but he was always saying, 'Let's take a few days and go somewhere.' And I would say, 'Oh, no, when I get back the work's piled up so bad,' and I put it off. Yes, I regret that.

"This has been a wonderful life and I can't really imagine leaving it. Even at retirement I know I'll still do it part time. Being Safari Jane has been good to me. It's been a beautiful way to communicate with people. I've been introduced to things I probably never would have known such as travel, photography, and working on radio and TV."

Nancy talked about the park. "I hoped the boys would come along into it, that we weren't building something that was going to come to a dead end. Because when you have live animals and you decide to retire, what happens to the animals? In fact, when Larry died I don't know what I would have done if I didn't have David here."

In November, after his father's death, David performed with an act of nine leopards. Eight years later, David said "I was only twenty-one when my dad died, so [I had] no time with him, such a small percentage of my adult life. I've changed so much since then. He was the best father."

Paul Pifer, who had grown up with the family told me, "Nancy is a gem. She always has been and always will be one of my favorite people. It couldn't have been easy being married to Jungle Larry. When he died it left a lot of pressure on her and I think, just like David, she's come out of it pretty secure and I sure applaud her for that."

Those that knew him said that Larry always had a big smile when he talked about his wife. He said that discovering Safari Jane was the biggest achievement of his career and that he would have been lost without her. Besides handling the administration for both complexes, she was one of the first female all-around animal trainers in the world. Long before it was the norm for a woman to head such a business, Nancy not only ran the huge

Tetzlaff enterprises but found time to raise her family and perform with the cats, too.

Nancy Runs the Parks

After her husband's death, Nancy spent more time on promotion and administration. The following summer, Jungle Larry's park entertained one million people at Cedar Point (20,000 in a day at times). Nancy worked twelve hours a day; a pace she still keeps at peak periods. She also serves on committees in the community and in 1993, was voted vice president of the Florida Attractions Association.

As chief executive officer of the parks, Nancy is in charge of operations, including marketing and advertising. "This is my 35th year in this business," Nancy said. "All these years I've never asked anyone to do a job that I have not done. Larry and I scrubbed every cage, groomed every animal—we *had* to do it all. We got up at 5:00 A.M., packed up animals, did our school shows, came back, fed, cleaned, put everybody to bed, then we took care of ourselves and ate and then checked them again at night. I don't feel I'm too good to do anything. I'm saying put the animals, company, and customers first. I see issues as black and white when it comes to safety and welfare of animals. There's usually the right way to do something and the wrong way and you can't deviate.

"As far as running the company, every department of Jungle Larry's comes through me, all purchasing, scheduling, planning. I've got a good crew out there, and as David has gotten older, he oversees almost all the animals for me. We have employees who've been here for eighteen years, like our Naples manager, Ralph Williams. When we come up with new projects like the boat ride we sit down together to plan it. They give me their proposals and cost estimates. The buck stops here whether we can do it or not."

Nancy makes decisions with the animals' and public's best interest in mind. When creating the petting-zoo area at the Naples park, Nancy wanted children to have a positive experience with animals. Separated by a wooden rail fence, a child can offer a cone of food pellets to a goat. The fence prevents the animal from climbing on a small child to get the food, as she has seen happen in some zoos. Nancy says it's important for a child to get to know the animal one-on-one, without fear of being mauled for the food he or she holds.

8.2 Tim, Nancy Jane, and David in front of a banyan tree in Naples, 1984.

Anyone who has had time to spend with Nancy learns that she has a wonderful sense of humor. When she had a large custom-made cage of snakes in her office years ago, if a sales representative overstayed, she would say, "It's time to exercise my snakes. You can stay if you'd like, or leave." She'd smile, "Whatever you're comfortable with." The salesperson would usually decide he'd sold enough.

Another way Nancy has fun on the job is being physically close to the cats' whose cage is right outside her office: caracals (Taffy, Tiffany, and Tyler) and servals (Geiger, Gabby, and Gina). Nancy lets them in through the window (when her office door is shut), but the animals never want to go back out. "If one is lying under my desk sleeping, I may slip out into my assistant's office briefly, and find that in five minutes they've awakened and while playing have cleared my desk. So I play fifty-two pick up. I'd have them in all day long, with the window open, but I couldn't leave the room. And getting them back outside—Taffy will go under the desk and picking her up is difficult. The only way I can get Geiger out is to take paper and wad up and toss it out; then he follows. But while that is happening, Taffy's bouncing back in."

Off the job, Nancy was among the founders of the Naples Corvette Club in 1976. She no longer has a Corvette, but says, "When I occasionally drive a friend's I remind myself I'm beyond that—getting down in, my back catches up with me. I enjoyed my car when I had it. Every time I see a Vette I drool for a minute in envy, but then cheer up and think, 'Wow! I used to have one!'"

Her interests are varied. Nancy also enjoys reading and music. Aside from trade journals, she likes to curl up with a good mystery when she can find the time. Her musical talents, fostered at a young age, lead her back to piano she played as a child.

She is also a deeply spiritual person who has an undying quiet faith in God. "He is the power in my life," she says.

8.3 Nancy Jane and husband, Bob Berens, at their wedding in 1987.

After Larry's death, Nancy began some new hobbies, including target shooting. Because of this interest, she met her present husband, Bob Berens, through a gun collector, Bob Dellete. It was a romance which began by mail. Nancy and Bob, a former sheriff in Stark County, Ohio began corresponding in August of 1987. They met a month later and were married December 31 that year.

Bob has been a tremendous support for Nancy and the family as they carry on the tradition of Jungle Larry.

PART THREE

Both David and I are animal rights advocates.
We advocate the right for animals to be healthy and
content and to have their minds stimulated.
—Pat White, animal trainer, the Yano Circus, Japan.

9

People Business: Public Relations at the Parks

I've never changed a human diaper, but when I was a teenager I changed a number of chimp diapers. At least human babies don't have fur like that. What a mess!
—Tim Tetzlaff

THROUGH THE YEARS, the Tetzlaffs have had their share of unusual incidents at the parks. After the 1991 article in *People* magazine, David received lots of complimentary mail, some of it unconventional: One couple even wrote to ask if David and his tigers could be at their wedding! Now there's a bridal party!

Humorous events are part of the history of the park. The family remembers that Larry had a great sense of humor and was able to make the most of unusual moments.

Art Kozlik likes to tell stories about his role as Larry's straightman during the snake show. "I don't think there was a line of corn we didn't know. We'd get in the arena with a fourteen- or fifteen-foot python or boa. It was my job to pick a good-looking woman out of the audience. The woman would stand on stage while Larry held the snake about five feet away from her. Larry said, 'One time a woman wanted to hold a snake and I had to revive her with mouth to mouth.' And I said, "Yeah, it took you forty minutes, didn't it? Bet her husband didn't like it.' Larry said, 'wasn't scared of him at all.' I said, 'No, he was only four foot-two inches! Larry was six foot-six inches, see? And he stood even taller with one-inch boot heels and a bush hat three inches above his head."

Larry often joked during his act. He might say of one of his big cats, "He likes beef. See? He's going after my calves." or "Notice I take off my watch. These guys are notorious for killing time."

Nancy, of course, was in the ring and added to the running gags. She would comment on her concern for Larry's safety in the arena but would say that after many years she finally realized that "the big cats eat beef, not a 'ham' like Larry, so I don't worry any more."

Nancy said, "Of course, Larry would turn and look at me, in wide-eyed surprise on his face, then laugh with the audience."

Even when Larry wasn't trying to be humorous, employees remembered funny incidents. Dick Gallagher, an employee who had worked at Jungle Larry's when he was a young man twenty years earlier said, "Back when this was Safari Island [Cedar Point], Larry had a dog. We brought over dog food for him, but the dog wouldn't eat it. So I parceled it into the water and the carp loved it. Larry saw this and grabbed the bag of dog food from me and said, 'Give me that! I'm going to sell it.' " Laughing, Dick said, "It became a big money-maker—dog food for fish."

Some humorous events have also occurred while television commercials were being taped, when the Tetzlaffs and animals were on live TV and while they were on media tours.

Nancy told me that while they were making a TV commercial for a car that used the tiger as its logo, they brought along Benji, a young tiger. "During the taping, a light on the set crashed from the ceiling to the floor. Startled, Benji took one step backward—into the side of the car. Its door caved in!" It obviously didn't look good for the strength of the car.

Another time, Nancy brought José, the cougar, to do a commercial for steel pipes at Panther Run in Youngstown, Ohio. "He had to come through steel tubing. I sent him down and he did great until he ran across a nest of rats. To get him out of there I really had to do some talking. He was having a ball."

Some of their appearances are part of planned tours. For a Cedar Point tour, the park administration will book one of their show personalities (such as the Tetzlaffs) for radio, TV, and newspaper interviews in nearby Cleveland, or any major city within several hundred miles. A Cedar Point representative sets the agenda, then travels with David or Nancy and discusses with them what is likely to be asked during the interview. In recent years for Cedar Point, David has taken leashed leopards, servals, caracals, and young tigers. The length of a trip is arranged so the animals have plenty of exercise, rest, and nourishment.

When you're working with animals, you never know exactly what to expect. Nancy said, "David will not appreciate my telling this, but he had a bad day in 1989 with Tiffany, the caracal, who I could do anything with. He took her on a media swing in Ohio with Melinda Huntley, a former Cedar Point media representative. With Tiffany spitting and fighting, David could barely get her out of the kennel carrier. Dave got *so* chewed up. In the TV studio, here's this big tiger and leopard trainer, and this little four-month-old, five-pound caracal—hissing, making mincemeat out of him. He was on the swing [tour] about sixteen hours, arriving home about midnight. I was waiting for him when he pulled up in the driveway and he said, 'Here, you can have her!' I opened the kennel door and said, 'Hi, Tiff!' and she came right to my arms and was loving me. Dave's expression said 'I give up!' "

Another time while staying in a hotel on a tour, Tiffany ripped up a bedspread and broke a lamp. David told me he left a photocopy of a picture of the caracal, put her paw print on it, and wrote, "Sorry about the mess, courtesy of your friendly neighborhood caracal." He also left money to cover the damage.

I met with Barb Colnar, a Cedar Point media representative who told me about a near fiasco during a media tour with Midnight, a little black panther [also called black leopard]. It was a long drive from Cedar Point to Indianapolis so "we'd have to let her out of her carrier every so often, to give her water and exercise. David had her on a leash and she'd stalk around and jump at me. I stepped away and her claws just missed me.

"When we got to the hotel it was late and I was starving. We checked in and David sneaked Midnight up the elevator to his room. He said, 'We'll go to dinner in ten minutes.' I went to my room. Twenty minutes later, I decided to go down the hall to see what was going on. David answered the door while on the phone and waved me in to the living area of the room. I stood watching the TV. Suddenly there was a huge, sharp pain in my butt. My natural reaction was to turn around and brush whatever it was away. Midnight had jumped from the floor and bitten me! She bounded across the room. We had gone to Fort Wayne two months before with that same cat. I could handle her back then and even play with her paws. But she'd grown considerably.

"She jumped in front of me and started playing like she used to. She started bounding from the floor up to my height, five feet, seven inches, toward my face. I crossed my hands in front of my face, and I fell backward. Midnight bit my thumb as hard as she could. That's when I screamed. Dave came in the room and took Midnight and locked her in the bathroom. He and I went out to eat. After dinner the bathroom was not in very good shape. We compensated the hotel.

"The next day our first TV [appointment] was an 8:00 A.M. taping. The TV host was very pregnant—looked like she could have gone any minute. She was sitting on my right and I was in the middle, with Dave on the left. The camera started and they rolled the credits—you could see it on the monitor. The TV host, Jane, said, 'We're here today with Barb Colnar and Dave Tetzlaff from Cedar Point.' No sooner did she say this when the leopard bolted, just jumped across the front of all three of us, across the set and Dave let go of the leash—he'd let go of it! He jumped up and dashed after her."

Barb noticed the curtains surrounding the studio and thought that if Midnight was in them, she would be gone. "The host was hyperventilating, and I stood up and got strangled by my mike. The cameraman was scared and ran out of the room. The camera kind of went off the set and followed the cat for a minute. Then it went down to the ground, so the out-take of this must have been hilarious. Dave made a diving leap to catch Midnight. He brought her back while I was trying to calm the host down, trying to laugh it off. Dave brought Midnight back to the left side of me. I still had my eye on that cat. Sure enough, I saw her jump and I made a sashay step to the right and she just missed me. Her claws caught my suit, making a loud RIPPPP that even drew the camera man's attention. I just brushed my skirt underneath me and sat down as if that hadn't happened, no big deal." Barb laughed. To this day, whenever she goes to the TV station they ask, "Whatever happened to that cat?"

Typically, though, the media tour is not humorous, but rather a relaxed time of educating the public about animals, Jungle Larry's, and Cedar Point.

Promotions

"We try to battle the tremendous lack of public knowledge about wildlife," said David. Education has been a strong component of the park's purpose ever since the early days of Jungle Larry. David or Nancy often appear with an animal at a community event or on TV to promote the park and various worthy causes. In the park's early days, Larry was always proud when a company filmed the park to show what the world might have looked like thousands of years ago before man started invading it. Through their own movie production company, Janlar (from Safari JANe and Jungle LARry), he produced films that were shown in schools and on TV.

Portions of movies or TV commercials needing jungle background were often made at Caribbean Gardens before 1969, when the Fleischmanns still managed the park. Larry continued with commercials for all sorts of products—everything from evening gowns to bathroom fixtures. Even today there are many requests from film and advertising companies to shoot at the park. Occasionally a company asks if Jungle Larry's has stock footage of a particular scene. If Jungle Larry's can provide it, they do. Nowadays, though, Nancy no longer has the time needed to devote to films.

One sunny summer day, in a restaurant near Cedar Point overlooking Lake Erie. Nancy told me about some amusing incidents about the park's experiences with film. "Years ago when we used to do more TV and movie work, the animals responded wonderfully to new situations. Larry did a commercial for a British car in a Miami botanical garden. The theme was a family lost in the jungle. One of our chimps, JJ, was to jump on the hood and beat on the windshield. He did it beautifully. To persuade the chimp to do it, Larry had people inside the car eating bananas and other food the chimp liked. Larry also had one of our pythons come out on a limb and hang down. The animals performed so well that they had everything in the first take.

"The promoter called us about two weeks later and said, 'Besides giving you your check, I'd like to thank you by giving you a black leopard cub.' That was Missy, Dave's first black leopard.

"Another time we did a photograph for American Greeting Card. We had our chimp in a business suit, sitting at a type-writer. To get the chimp to type, Larry put little goodies on the typewriter keys. The chimp would touch the key and lick off the goodie quickly, while getting more goodies on the other hand to touch to his lip and keep both hands going.

"In 1985 we did a takeoff on a Bartles & Jaymes commercial to promote the park, in which two chimps, JJ and JR, are 'talk-ing.' To get them to keep moving their lips and look like they were talking we kept giving them Bit•O•Honey. You can do many kind things like that to get the effects you want."

Through the years, Jungle Larry's parks have had promotions and discounts affiliated with National Airlines, Eastern Airlines, General Mills Cheerios among others. Other commercials since then have been for London Fog and for Amdro fire ant killer.

I talked to Nancy and David about work for commercials. He told me Jungle Larry's gets at least six or seven phone calls every month asking them to take an animal on location for a commer-cial, but he refers the callers to other people. David said, "We don't have the time and resources to fly to New York or wher-ever. I could make one thousand to three thousand dollars a day on a set, but I'm too committed here. It's heartbreaking to miss that income—because we are not publicly funded—but I can't be in two places at once."

Nancy added that the work can be hard on the animals, and routinely transporting animals is difficult. "For the animals that could be flown, we'd need to have special cages made. The big cats could not go by air so you'd have to have a truck and trailer with heating, air conditioning, and a freezer for the meat."

Since Larry's death, Nancy and David have continued to carry on the tradition of opening the park to various worthy groups to help them raise funds. In 1987 Jungle Larry's actively promoted literacy by giving matching dollars (from park visitors' coupons) to Project Literacy in U.S. (PLUS), an organization that teaches thousands of Americans to read. In another project, Jungle Larry's presented a show for five hundred needy children, and provided free box lunches, thanks to contributions from several local busi-nesses.

The Tetzlaffs have also created special offers based on Ameri-can themes, such as National Dental Week—Larry brushed a tiger's teeth! Another time the park honored Native Americans at a day-long festival at which Seminole food, paintings, beadwork, basketry, and woodworking were featured throughout the park.

In the early 1990s, Jungle Larry's began a Halloween custom of helping Girls, Inc., raise money. Their theme was "Boo in the Zoo." Nancy said, "The group had their own exhibits all around the park. Frankenstein came alive out of his coffin placed in the Orchid Cathedral and went over to kiss his bride and she rose— all with strobe lighting. Then they walked onto the tram. 'Headhunters' at Lagoon Loop screamed and got on the train. They even had a witches' cauldron setting on dry ice."

The Tetzlaffs have always sought to inform the public about animals. When David or Nancy take small animals on TV to promote an upcoming event at the park, it's not only for public relations, but to educate as well. The personal appearances, which began with Larry, have continued to this day. Years ago Jungle Larry was on the "Mike Douglas Show" and the "Today Show" many times with various reptiles and with the tiglon cubs. Recently Nancy and David individually have been on local shows.

Nancy told me about the time she went on television in 1986 with an elephant. "When Hadari was small we took her back and forth to Ohio two summers. I had a small, blue horse trailer that she'd be in, pulled by my van. We took her to Cleveland for TV that summer. She went in the studio so sweetly, stepping over these big cables. Hadari had always sat on the aluminum tub (as a trick) since she was small.

"The emcee sat down on a park bench in the TV studio. Young Hadari promptly went over and sat on the bench beside the emcee and stole the show."

In 1989 David took a six-month-old white tiger, Taurus, to the Naples Beach Hotel. "I had five white tigers here on loan from Josip Marcan. To advertise the park, I just took one of them to the hotel and talked about him, let people take pictures of him, but not standing with him or touching him. I never let people touch other peoples' animals.

"But public relations is important. I just did a TV thing yesterday and [thought], 'All right, I'll do it and let me get back to work.' I tend to get depressed with all that stuff. I'd rather stay here with the animals.

9.1 David completing an eleven leopard over-the-bar and sit-up.

"Gebel-Williams was on 'Johnny Carson' five times, and it's nice getting attention like that, but a lot of time the animals get degraded in situations like that. I don't want a comedian making jokes about my cats. It takes away from our purpose."

A Leopard Fight Stopped

A particularly upsetting and discouraging event in David's career occurred in 1991, when he had to break up a fight during the leopard act. He had begun the act as usual and the troupe had performed without any problem. Suddenly, with only four tricks to go before the finale, one leopard, without provocation, attacked another member of the act.

The leopards were obediently waiting while David moved the pedestals into place for the next behavior. Suddenly, Benjamin, a sleek eleven-year old leopard, jumped off his assigned seat and attacked another male leopard, Ceylon. This was not play. Ben was intent on eliminating Ceylon. David immediately picked up the throat fork and ran to stop the fight. If David had failed, he knew he could have had one or more dead leopards, or he, him-self, might be injured or killed. Ben had his jaws around Ceylon's neck when David used the wooden throat fork to break up the fight. When David got Ben off Ceylon, Ceylon ran to the other side of the arena and Ben, eager to provoke more action, jumped on Ceylon's seat. David recognized this as defiance and knew that Ben was positioning himself to attack again. David rapped Ben on the head once with the throat fork (which had been broken in the earlier mêlée) while commanding him verbally to go back to his seat. "Seat!" ordered David.

Ben, recognizing David's authority, returned to his own pedestal and was then sent out of the arena. David checked Ceylon over and found only minor abrasions and some blood oozing from his nose. More frightened than hurt, Ceylon was comforted and treated for his wounds after the rest of the cats left the arena.

The audience wildly applauded David. Although people probably knew David had been in danger of getting in the middle of a cat fight, they may not have realized that Ceylon's life was in more jeopardy because leopards generally fight to kill. When David stopped the attack he may well have saved Ceylon's life.

As a credit to David's training skills, the rest of the cats stayed on their seats during the skirmish. If they had not been so well-trained, David might have had eleven cats involved in one of the biggest cat fights of the century.

Unfortunately the incident, which David had handled so well, ended up with national television coverage that gave the wrong impression of the event. Someone in the crowd had videotaped the incident and evidently thought the footage of the fight might be interesting to newscasters. A local television station accepted the tape but rather than showing it in its original form, edited the tape not only to make it falsely appear that David had struck Ben more than once, but changed the order of events to make it appear that the fight occurred *after* David had reprimanded Ben. That totally inaccurate version of the incident was repeated, perhaps to create some "news" for the station.

As a result of showing the blatantly mis-edited version, which added the repeated blows, a complaint was filed against David with the USDA (which oversees the care and treatment of exotic animals) and other organizations. Fortunately, a local agent of the USDA had seen the original version, and knew that the broadcast version had been significantly altered. As the result of his testimony and a very thorough investigation, David was completely exonerated of any wrong doing!

Jungle Larry's considered pressing civil charges against the TV station for editing the tape and misrepresenting the facts but, after consultations with their attorneys and with a few other parks who'd been in similar situations, decided against such action. David had handled a difficult situation—the leopard fight—with the utmost skill and professionalism. It was painful to have the episode taken out of context and portrayed falsely.

Jim Cole, who knows animal trainers and training around the world said, "I called the USDA representative and told him that David is first class with animals. It was just an unfortunate incident. The leopard was trying to kill the other leopard and that's the only thing David could do at the time. Other animal trainers I talked to felt the same way. He saved the leopard's life, you know? He felt bad about that incident, but what can you do? Those things happen. He still feels bad about it.

"David is an animal rights activist in his own sense because he's so conscientious about the animals. Some circuses and some people in the business shouldn't have animals, and David's very critical of them. So am I. But David knows his stuff," said Cole.

Accountability and Safety

"For a park our size you can plan on one full day, eight hours a week, just to work on paperwork for permits. For a small company, that's expensive, but it's the cost of doing business," Nancy told me.

Visitors to both parks are so intrigued by the wildlife, the animal acts and landscaping that it is easy to walk away without understanding how much work goes on behind the scene to provide such an exciting and smooth-running operation. There is much more to the parks than what is seen during a casual visit. For example, both the proper care of the animals and the safety of employees is extremely important. Jungle Larry himself helped developed some of the regulations for the care of wild animals, and the family makes sure that all employees are well prepared to take safety precautions for their own well-being.

Like all parks that feature wild animals, Jungle Larry's deals with government permits and regular inspections as well as self-imposed safety procedures. Because Jungle Larry's is so careful with its employees and animals, it has had only five minor accidents since the park opened in 1969.

Facilities that keep wild animals in captivity and are open to the public must have government permits from both the USDA and the U.S. Fish and Game Commission. Once or twice a year representatives of these departments perform unscheduled inspections of the licensed facility.

Nancy keeps detailed records. She gave her pencil a tap thoughtfully and said, "For each animal I keep a file from the date of birth or acquisition, a history of its life with us. If the animal is sold that history moves on to the next owner, or if it dies, I record the reason for death. We do an autopsy at nearly every death. We always perform it on the endangered species."

When David and I discussed other government regulations, he said that although autopsy is not required by any government agency, he feels it should be required on animals who die of anything other than old age. "You don't have to autopsy," he said. "That's why some dirty, illegal things go on in this field. When a big cat gets over eighteen years old, it dies from old age; the body just wears down. If it's a young animal, an eight, nine, or ten-year-old that dies, any responsible person is going to want to know why."

Employee and Visitor Safety

The 100-page manual of procedures contains information for the safety of animals, visitors, and employees. An example of a rule applying to the show department is this: When exercising animals in the arena, never leave the animals unsupervised. David explained the reason for this precaution. "Leopards could hurt each other; someone could conceivably climb the safety fence and stick a hand through the arena cage. Even when no visitors are in the park, we follow the procedures as if someone were here. My father taught safety first. We don't leave much to chance that way."

In the training manual, the Tetzlaffs stress care of the animals and common sense concerning employees' safety. Examples include checking each animal in a keeper's care at the beginning of the shift. This includes making a nose count and completing daily records of animals' appetites and behavior; noting any irregularities; checking a yard before entering, making sure no animals are in the enclosure; using water buckets only for animals' water—not for disinfectant. Hoses are to be kept neatly coiled, for safety and appearance. Employees are asked to conserve water—sweep floors of debris before using the hose.

Other employees are not allowed to pet animals. The employee manual of procedures stresses that all animals on the grounds are dangerous and are not trained for or used to being petted. "Never take a chance thinking you might be able to pet an animal and get away with not getting injured. Wild animals are much quicker than we are and they are aware of your daily routines. If you, for example, pass by a cat or monkey's enclosure each day at the same place, that animal is aware of the distance and knows how far it has to reach out to get you." The employees respect the animals, and the Tetzlaffs' wishes.

As part of their education for working at the park, employees are advised that even wearing a ring can be hazardous.

Nancy explained, "Larry learned this the hard way: he almost lost a finger working with his wedding band on. For employees' safety, we prefer they do not wear rings."

Nancy and David have a thirty-minute staff meeting each week to communicate updated procedures, and inform the employees of progress on any new construction projects. Afterwards, an assistant writes up and distributes a one-page summary of the meeting to each employee. I had the opportunity to read a number of the transcripts which gave me an excellent picture of the behind the scenes operations. During one meeting in 1992, David told the tram drivers, "If you are between rides and watching the tiger show, do not initiate applause. I want to know if the audience likes the show and weren't just led into applause." In another meeting, Nancy told employees not to inform park visitors of animals' names. If only a fraction of those visitors called out the animals' names, the animals would be disturbed hearing their names shouted at them one hundred times a day.

If an employee does have a problem, the CB radio on each cart can be used to call co-workers for help. CB radios must be on all day. Employees are told to be alert for anyone trying to reach them. For a major emergency parks commonly use a code to let their employees know of danger and to implement the appropriate plan. I've heard that one circus played "Stars and Stripes" to alert employees of an emergency.

I was told that if there is an emergency at Jungle Larry's, an alarm sounds along with a code that tells the staff which area the problem is in. Nancy said, "The highest degree of warning is if an animal is loose. We have a training procedure for that, so employees know what to do. If an animal has escaped or if an employee is in trouble with an animal everyone immediately responds. Thankfully, the alarm hasn't gone off in a long time."

In all of its years of operation, Jungle Larry's has had so few visitor incidents that all of them can be described in a page or two. Jungle Larry's accident record is exemplary, although the park in Naples has more than 100,000 visitors a year and the Cedar Point operation, in later years, averaged one million.

One evening in 1974, long after Jungle Larry's had closed for the day, a young man climbed over a perimeter fence surrounding the park. He went to a lion's cage, stuck his hand in, was bitten, then left the park quickly. He was charged with trespassing after a deputy responded to a call to the Naples Community Hospital, where the intruder was being treated for lacerations to his right hand.

Only twice were regular visitors injured by an animal at the park. The first, and most serious, occurred in the winter of 1970 after the presentation of the year-old tiglons. While the caretaker took one of the two tiglons to its cage, the other tiglon was briefly alone in the performance arena. A four- or five-year-old child climbed through the guard rail and put his hand through the bars to feed the tiglon some animal crackers. When the child reached through the bars, the tiglon clawed the child's face. Larry and Wally, the manager, were nearby, but not fast enough to prevent the incident. Fortunately, the child was not badly injured, but the Tetzlaffs were devastated. They quickly installed chain link safety fences, which have successfully prevented any repetition of the incident.

Human error is the weakness in the most sophisticated animal enclosures. In the 1970s Midnight, a six-year-old black leopard weighing eighty-five pounds escaped and was out of her cage for twelve hours. Apparently the latch of the door was not secured. Midnight, raised in captivity, was confused by her freedom and roamed less than three hundred feet from her cage. The staff tried to entice Midnight back to her cage with her favorite dish—chicken meat, but she had denned up during the heat of the day. Finally, a deputy sheriff shot her with a dart from a tranquilizer gun as she tried to return to the security of her cage. She was taken to the animal hospital for observation before being returned to her cage. Jungle Larry's director and another employee stayed with her until 3:00 A.M. to make sure she didn't have a reaction to the tranquilizer.

And then there was Sabrina, who decided she wanted to play with children. One afternoon in January of 1987 David was exercising the seven-month-old leopard cub when she slipped through her enclosure and scratched a six-year-old girl who was jumping with a group of children. Apparently the cat wanted to join them in their games. The girl had some scratches and a puncture and was treated at the hospital and released. The park quarantined the cub for a few weeks to be sure it had no diseases that might harm the child. It didn't.

In May of 1987, the trainer John Illig's four-year-old show lioness, Gobi, slipped out when a lock malfunctioned. Nancy remembers that Gobi walked out of her cage and trainers used a tranquilizer dart to subdue her. No one was hurt, and she was back in her cage before the park opened.

David spoke to me about safety. "If a cat gets loose that's the number two scariest thing. Number one is an animal getting hold of somebody. It's always human error. When Midnight was out years ago, people walked right by looking for her and didn't find her. If that were to happen now, I'd find the animal, because I know where a leopard would go and know what it's going to do.

"I check locks twice every day before I go home. Many employees say that I check too much! I'm simply paranoid. Most cases the cats are scared if they're out. People think, *poor thing in a cage.* But that's what the animals know. It's their life. They don't know the outside."

Concerning safety, Nancy recalled, "Years ago we used to get a kick out of the agencies' inspectors saying, 'Larry, if something goes wrong in that arena, you are going to shoot the cat aren't you?' Larry would say, 'Sure, there's a man behind there with a rifle that's going to shoot out there in the arena with the whole audience in front of them!' Get realistic. You can't do that. You can't even rely on tranquilizer guns, because it takes the drug between five and twenty minutes to work. Films always show the gun being fired and the animal going right down. It doesn't work that way. The only way it will happen quicker is if you give them an overdose, to kill. Tranquilizers take time. If an animal got loose we'd try to save him, if it's a situation where we could. But we have live ammunition too. We do feel a responsibility to

the public and we have the rule that if an animal ever leaves this premises the orders are bring the animal down. Don't ever let him hurt anyone." Happily, the two escapees they've had over the years never got off the property.

10

Outlook on Animals in Captivity

People have so many misconceptions about this business. My reason for wanting this book to appear is to get the word out about the real situation.

—David Tetzlaff

THE SUBJECT of how animals are treated by people is often an emotional one. Not all wild animals in captivity are fortunate enough to be raised, trained, and cared for by parks or zoos which are committed to high standards of care and treatment as well as conservation.

Early "tamers" of captured lions and tigers often attempted to break the animals' spirits by force. Even recently, sadistic or unaware trainers have mistreated big cats.

Public outcry about such abuse has led to government regulation. Facilities that keep wild animals in captivity and are open to the public must have government permits from and be inspected once or twice per year by both the USDA and state Fish and Game Commissions. These inspections are unscheduled, intending to evaluate the facility as it really operates. Of the thousands of unscheduled inspections annually, only a few sites are found to be abusive, such as the case David recounts: "Government officials took some cats away from somebody up in Ohio one summer recently. The guy had eight lions and tigers; the cats were anemic and emaciated, and the freezer had [only] forty pounds of chicken backs. That's enough to feed those cats for one day! Those animals were starving! Look at our freezer! We've got 20,000 pounds of food in that freezer right now. This guy had forty pounds. To me a clean cage, fresh water, good food, that's the minimum animals need, and a lot of animals don't even get that [at some places]."

10.1 Nancy Jane holding eight-week-old caracal and serval cubs in 1991.

Despite mandated government control, the USDA inspection staff is limited, and consequently conditions may remain bad for some animals in some locations. David continued, "Some government agencies have more than enough people to inspect facilities, and other places there's not enough staff. Our inspector in Ohio is responsible for half the state of Ohio, part of Pennsylvania and part of West Virginia. One person is supposed to look over hundreds of places in that large an area. No way. There's no way."

To add to the problem, many practices are unethical or questionable but not illegal. David speaks out against any individual or organization that doesn't put animals first. "In 1994—in an animal-conscious age—some people still approve of declawing. If some of these people are trainers, that doesn't mean they're doing things right and that I have to like them even though we're in the same business. Some people say that declawing is the professional thing to do. 'We're here to do a job, not to get hurt.' I don't buy that. If I get hurt doing the job it's my fault, but I'm not going to mess up an animal."

Outraged, David continued, "I met a guy recently who showed me pictures of a cougar he has. This cat's declawed front and back. It's got its canines out. What's that? That's not a beautiful animal any more. It's a cripple. You're not being a real animal person when you start hacking up your cats."

Activist Reaction

Unfortunately, animal abuse has not been confined to acts and shows. Animals used in research have been neglected and mistreated. Some caretakers would undernourish them; some industries would exploit them. For example some cosmetics companies tested their products for eye sensitivity by putting chemicals in animals' eyes. Some researchers induced diseases in animal models in order to test "cures."

The public became concerned about animal welfare as early as 1883 because of the numerous kinds and instances of abuse and neglect, and formed organizations such as the American Antivivisection Society. Various groups strongly believe in commendable goals such as good care for animals, no unnecessary testing on animals, and no mistreatment.

Some issues addressed by animal groups are more controversial. One such question is medical research. Those in favor of using animals for research claim that medical advances for humans, such as vaccines and cancer treatments (surgery, radiation, and chemotherapy) would not have been developed without animal research. Animals are tested because many of their fundamental cellular processes, such as those in genes and organs, are similar to peoples'. For example, chronic toxicity studies help determine cancer risk from a given substance.

On the other hand, dissenters argue that such studies have limited use. Even among humans, the variables of ethnicity, age, sex, smoking, drinking, and so on, obscure results. Does an animal study extrapolate to humans? Moreover, animal activists have protested that many studies go too far. Although the vast majority of scientists do not want their animals abused, animals have sometimes been shocked, injected, probed, operated on, and denied sleep, food, or water. Activists have argued that alternative research methods such as tissue cultures, physiochemical techniques, clinical and epidemiological studies, and mathematical and computer modeling are often available.

When I talked with David about the subject of how some animals are mistreated in other situations, his usual reticence was replaced by agitation. "Years ago [people] committed terrible atrocities against animals, doing experiments on them before there was anesthesia, nailing them to boards and cutting them open when they were alive—it just makes you ill that your ancestors did something like that. It's detailed in the book, *Rose-Tinted Menagerie,* which tears apart zoos, aquariums, everything."

Animal activists have helped make the public more aware of atrocities committed against animals in some laboratories and have forced changes in former standard practices. For example, many cosmetics companies no longer use animals in testing their products (such as for eye sensitivity). And, although people once needed animal skins to stay warm, synthetic fur is now widely used instead.

Most people want better lives for animals, and continuation of the species. Probably most of us share goals for animals that involve compassion and principled behavior. To achieve those goals, we still need to listen to all points of view while avoiding overreaction and inflexible attitudes.

Frank Thompson (former zoo director in Jacksonville, Florida) hopes for "an averaging out of attitudes. The animal-rights people have some legitimate cause for complaint, because there have been some people that have badly abused their animals. There still are a few—relatively few, but still a few. But we all know that this isn't true of everyone. There are people like David who truly love their animals and who'd do anything and everything to see that their animals are happy and well cared for. The problem with some people in the animal-rights movement is that they are painting everyone with the same brush and this simply is neither fair nor accurate."

Tim told me, "Activists are getting very involved and they've got some good ideas, but a lot of times the people are too far removed from the industry to know what they're talking about. People are misled into thinking they know what's best for animals, when they've never worked in a zoo, never been directly involved."

Tim thinks that good intentions often become misguided efforts. "The majority of people who support activists love animals and want to help make animals' lives better. But some of the organizations go after the wrong things—side issues [such as eliminating pets] instead of the main issues [such as ensuring that endangered species do not become extinct]."

In *BBC Wildlife* magazine (December 1987), Desmond Morris wrote, "The human population of Africa is doubling with every generation. This means that in sixty years' time, when our children have reached retiring age, the wild animals of Africa will have only a quarter of the space they now enjoy. And so it will go on until Africa, like Europe, will have nearly eliminated all its large fauna. In a few centuries, wild animals will survive only in zoos, because that is all the space they will have left, anywhere. So perhaps we should start now to plan our 'ideal zoos' rather than be emotional about the concept of captivity. Then we will be ready for the ever more crowded future."

Ironically, activist organizations that oppose zoos (rather than opposing the abuse occurring in a minority of them) are actually opposing the survival of the endangered animals. Human overpopulation and wilderness destruction may make zoos the last chance for some species' continuation. Zoos care for more individuals of some species than remain in the wild.

The best zoos are not jails for animals, but havens—considering that many, if not most of them, were born and raised in captivity. Aside from protecting species from extinction, the best zoos and parks also provide natural surroundings, good food and veterinary care, which lead to contentment and longer lives. Another advantage is that in such an environment, visitors, especially children, may learn about animals and grow to appreciate their needs. Education leads to understanding and sensitivity, which in turn promote an attitude of concern and conservation.

Ron Whitfield, a tiger and lion trainer at Marine World/Africa USA in northern California, is a strong proponent of education, who spends time after his performances answering questions for audiences of three thousand. One of his beliefs is that in some ways, animal businesses are even better for the animals than are zoos. He finds that "If cats don't work, they're bored. [Inactive animals] don't act as well adjusted as if you stimulate their minds, [whereas show cats] have something to look forward to besides just being on display." David agrees, as do his tigers, who often cuddle up to him for petting as an apparent expression of their pleasure after a show.

Overall, the majority of zoo personnel and animal trainers care deeply for their charges. Effective animal advocates, from within these industries and from activist groups, have helped correct insensitive and inhumane practices as we all have gradually become more aware of animal needs. This long process of raising consciousness involves both opposition and understanding, and the best progress is made when all parties listen and respond. Whitfield's optimism is instructive: "I think animal-rights people are putting a lot of pressure on all of us [trainers] to reevaluate  what we're doing and how we're doing it." He and the many other animal workers I spoke with all expressed hope that activists and the public will continue to learn more about the realities of animal care, contentment, and survival.

11

A Look to the Future

The American wild animal trainer may be an endangered species himself.
—Joanne Joys in *Wild Animal Trainer in America*

THROUGHOUT THIS BOOK we have seen that although most trainers and handlers have been kind and dedicated, a few owners of wild animals have abused them. As a result, there has been much more concern in recent years about the treatment of captive animals. This has led to increased government regulation, more public attention, and altered animal entertainments. Much of this is for the good, and legitimate animal trainers welcome the changes. For example, present-day animal shows tend to exhibit more natural behaviors in the "tricks" and often feature a large educational component. Presumably the immediate future will show continued trends to respect and protect these animals.

As the public is better educated, they may support efforts to preserve the natural habitat of wild animals to avoid extinction of at least some species. For others, it may already be too late.

Nancy and many others are concerned that their grandchildren's grandchildren may never see animals in this country. Without the help of zoos, extinction of some species would already be complete. Because animal people are helping to save whole species, this role may gain prominence. Perhaps the beliefs and attitudes of animal workers, animal activists, and the general public will converge as we all become more informed.

When I asked Frank Thompson how zoos may change in the next ten years, he replied, "I think they'll change much as they have in the past ten years—attention to proper housing, proper care, and proper diets.

"Certainly not much attention will be paid to the silliness of animal rights extremists, I would hope. Such people are no more qualified to tell a legitimate zoo with a full complement of curatorial staff, vets and animal behaviorists, how to handle animals than I am to fly a rocket ship to the moon."

David predicts that governments may intervene further, at least in small businesses. "The people with the backyard stuff are going to get regulated out sooner or later, even though some are doing a good job." Author Joanne Joys states that government standards may be expanded to include licensing trainers rather than the institution or attraction where they work. Presently, animal training has no standards for competence, qualifications, testing, or ethics, as do those in the legal and medical professions. Even in those professions, though, a certificate does not guarantee expertise.

David is sometimes pessimistic about the future of animal acts; once he commented, "We will see the end of the animal act in my lifetime. It might even be within ten years. Already four or five cities in Canada have banned animal acts. Another city in Florida just did it."

Even if animal acts endure, with demonstrations of natural behaviors having taken the place of displays of unnatural stunts, the current trend of increasing education seems likely to continue, with a greater emphasis on learning about animal needs, behaviors, and realities. This will likely be true in both zoos and private businesses.

Because they lack the public support for animal care, businesses have to direct much of their own funds into animal care. Dr. Noble finds the effort "remarkable" that Jungle Larry's staff put into maintaining and improving the park, and keeping the animals healthy. "It's much better, I think, than some of the city-supported zoos in other parts of the country. It's a big undertaking and they do an excellent job."

An Exciting Future

Jungle Larry's Zoological Park in Naples has more than 180 animals and three thousand subtropical plants. Rather than simply maintaining the park, the Tetzlaffs are always undertaking new projects, many solely for the animals' benefit. The animals' care comes first. The cages' concrete floors are regularly disinfected and sanitized, not merely rinsed. The staff is installing wooden floors with air space underneath so the wood will be easier on the big cats' feet. Also, the land use at the park is determined by the animals' needs.

Some planned park improvements will involve new exhibits. In one recent addition, different kinds of monkeys and lemurs were added, each of these primate species being given its own spacious island in Lake Victoria. In early 1994 the Tetzlaffs had already bought some animals and bred even more. They bought two gibbons and a few black and white ruffed lemurs and white fronted lemurs.

11.1 Ralph Williams, long-time manager at the Naples park.

The Tetzlaffs have always bred big cats. Between January and May of 1994 thirteen cubs were born, including tigers, servals, and caracals. Sometimes the breeding may help to preserve rare species. For example, Nancy hopes to help perpetuate the white tiger: "Some of our Bengal tigers carry the white gene, so we hope to have a white tiger born here someday. We have good blood lines. We don't breed anyone who's related."

On the park's fortieth anniversary celebration in February of 1994 the Tetzlaffs and park manager Ralph Williams revealed plans for new projects. Presenting drawings of the plans to the invited guests, David talked about the zoological addition: "One cat species, the clouded leopard (which has large dark cloud-shaped markings) is so rare that no one even knows how many are in the wilds of southern China, Sumatra, and Borneo. We don't even know whether these cats prefer to hunt in forests or in the open. They're believed to eat birds, monkeys, pig, cattle, goats, and deer but nothing is known about their social system. Only a handful exist in captivity. During 1994 a pair from the Buffalo Zoological Gardens of New York will be lent to Jungle Larry's, where a forested part of the park is being prepared to house them. The exhibit will have an alcove where people can get close to a portion of the exhibit. These fifty- to sixty-pound cats will have water running over rocks, along with a net-like roof, because they like to jump."

The Tetzlaffs use environment-friendly products, such as the indestructible, recycled plastic logs (which don't breed bacteria as do the wooden ones) for the big cats. Jungle Larry's also actively recycles, stockpiling the elephant manure, aging it a year and bringing it back as natural fertilizer for the plants.

Carrying on His Father's Tradition

Based on the respect of his peers, David has already earned a reputation as an outstanding trainer. Jim Cole told me, "If I were to list great cat trainers in the business today, it'd be Josip Marcan, James Clubb, Gunther Gebel-Williams, and David Tetzlaff [not necessarily in that order]." Pat White feels that "[His future is] up to David. He certainly has the incentive, drive, and talent to pursue this as far and as long as he chooses."

Unless the extremists among animal activist groups are successful in banning all animals from captivity, David's training skills will likely please crowds for many years. Fortunately, most people who care about animals are more moderate and understand the benefit of zoos. David observed, "The public cares about the cat show. . . if you took it away people would [be displeased]. On my day off they're unhappy; even though there's plenty to see in this park without the cat show, we've had people not come in because the cats weren't working."

David is justifiably proud of his accomplishments with leopards; his former act involving seventeen of these difficult cats may be unsurpassed, but he says it's irrelevant now. "I'm told that I created one of the best leopard acts ever. [But] I've done it; so I don't want to do it anymore. I look at all the tricks those leopards did—so many different things. There's a lot to be proud of, but it's history.

"I trained leopards for my own pleasure. Now I've got past the stage where [my work] is for me." People in the business agree that leopards are craftier, more dangerous, and more difficult to train, but that the American public is more impressed with tigers because of their great size. Now David says, "I want to be a good tiger trainer. Tigers are for the people. I could spend my entire life with tigers and I don't think Americans would get bored with it."

11.2 David poses with a young tiger in the Naples park.

11.3 Family photo, 1983.

Never satisfied, David wants to be innovative. He plans to expand his tiger act to eight animals, adding new tricks as well. He'd also like to acquire a snow leopard. "I can pick every leopard I have up in my arms, but I only had two or three I could put up on my shoulders. It's a totally different feel for the cat. So if I could do a snow leopard shoulder-carry at the end of the tiger act that would be pretty awesome. I might even impress myself again." He has also hinted that he wants to put together a mixed ("harmony") act, but so far he's not telling anyone, even his mother, which other species he has in mind.

Given his devotion to and enthusiasm for working with animals, one might wonder at David's doubt about the value of his own occupation: "One of my friends is a nurse and another is a fireman; they're doing something to help people. The world doesn't need an animal trainer. The guy who puts car parts on Ford Escorts in Detroit, or somebody in Iowa growing food to feed the country is more important than me. Trainers aren't doing anything to change the world."

But this attitude is easily reconciled with David's real motivation, which may differ from that of most trainers. "I don't care as much about having a show as I do about having a natural environment and informing people about the animals. The one thing that I do justify in myself is letting people know about the environmental end of things, which I try to bring across to people in here."

I asked Tim to predict David's next ten years. Tim sees in his brother a continuation of their father's care for animals: "It's what my Dad did; I expect to see more of my Dad coming out in David. He's moving more into education, so I expect more lecture formats, so that the public gets a better understanding of the animals and animal issues."

I also asked several respected professionals in the field, including other trainers, to speculate about David's future. The consensus is that since David is a caring trainer who articulates the truth, he will help educate the public about animal realities. Roy Wells predicts that in ten years, David "will still be working with the animals and continuing to educate the public so they get a good knowledge of the animals, instead of just out there showing himself as a trainer. He shows how man can work with the animals. He's one of the better spokesmen that animal trainers and handlers have."

Wells and others also think that David will eventually manage Jungle Larry's.

Currently David helps his mother with decision-making and has various firm opinions about directions for the park, although his desires conflict. "I could make a full-time job just managing the zoo, having ideas for new exhibits and new animals. I'd like to see us grow. I've got a lot of visions for the park but I want to be a trainer too and am split in half all the time."

It has been said that the best indicator of long-term success is character. Of the dozens of highly reputable friends, acquaintances, and colleagues with whom I talked, all showed a remarkable respect, often admiration, for David and his family. Given the Tetzlaffs' strength and character, whatever fortune has in store

for them, on balance, it should be rewarding. Since character breeds character, they will also continue to uplift those around them. As I have attempted to relate in this book, their benevolence has been both spiritual and concrete.

Appendix A

A History
of the Parks

Jungle Larry's is the longest running animal act at any amusement park in the world.   —Cedar Point press release, 1992

WITH A RARE combination of talent, knowledge and showmanship, it's little wonder that Larry Tetzlaff's career led from the scientific work with snakes to the creation of two outstanding public parks where exotic animals could be seen, understood, and enjoyed.

From Larry's early years in Kalamazoo, Michigan at the Reptilium to the animal compound at Chippewa Lake, near Cleveland, Ohio, and from his appearances at zoos and television, Larry gained the experience and credibility in his field that led to the success of the Cedar Point and Naples parks. He understood what interested the public and knew that once they visited the park, people could be educated as they were entertained. Public awareness could help conservation and might keep various specious from becoming extinct.

Success did not happen overnight. And as with many people who served their country during the war, he had to start over with his business contacts when he completed his military career. As he rebuilt his connections in the world of animal training, he was also building a collection of animals.

Fortunately, by the time Larry's zoo of fifty wild animals and rare birds outgrew his Chippewa Lake compound in 1965, the management of Cedar Point Amusement Park invited him to bring his zoo to the park. The contract, appropriately, was endorsed with an unusual signature: Coco, an African lion cub, added his inky paw print next to Larry's on the "dotted lion." So began a wonderful three-decade association between the Tetlzaff family and the world-famous amusement park. Cedar Point on Lake Erie was an ideal summer location for the animal shows, and displays of reptiles, wild animals, and rare birds.

At Cedar Point, Larry, Nancy, and their staff presented trained chimps, elephants, tigers, alligators, and lions to more than 600,000 visitors each summer.

The Tetzlaffs also trained chimps, zebras, antelopes, and elands for television shows such as "Cowboy in Africa" and "Daktari" and trained and sold various animals to Hollywood studios. Two of their hyenas appeared in the film, *Dr. Doolittle*.

A.1 Safari Jane and Jungle Larry with elephants and llama at Naples, about 1980.

Each year the Tetzlaffs made improvements to the Cedar Point park for the benefit of their animals and for the public's convenience and safety. In 1966, Jungle Larry's was the third zoo in the United States to build a "World of Darkness" tunnel for nocturnal animals, where red lights were used to simulate night so animals would be active for people viewing them during daylight hours. At closing, white lights would trigger the animals' sleep cycle. In May 1975, they undertook a $50,000 renovation—a large domed pavilion for a "Circus Africa" show. The Charter-Sphere Dome was eighty feet in diameter. The seating capacity for the tiger arena was about five hundred people, but on peak days in Ohio in July and August, sometimes David found as many people standing as sitting.

A.2 Jungle Larry working with young lions.

Between shows, visitors could follow the paved trail through the wooded grounds where animals and reptiles were displayed, including tigers, leopards, servals, parrots, wallabies (a marsupial that looks like a small kangaroo), and snakes.

Art Kozlik, the manager in Ohio (until his retirement at the conclusion of the 1994 season), trained hybrid wolves (one-eighth malamute, seven-eighths McKensey and Arctic wolf), demonstrating their natural behaviors.

Cedar Point—The Amazement Park—ranks with major entertainment parks in the nation. *Money* magazine rated the nation's top ten theme parks by gate admittance and Cedar Point makes the list.

A.3   Art Kozlik, longtime manager of Cedar Point operations and his trained wolf.

Jungle Larry's Zoological Park in Caribbean Gardens in Naples, Florida, is located on the site of a botanical gardens founded in 1919 by Dr. Henry Nehrling, a noted professor of botany and ornithology. He created a "garden of solitude" on his initial ten-acre plot with plants native to tropical and subtropical West Indies, Africa, Asia, and Australia. Within a few years Nehrling had more than three thousand thriving specimens. After his death in 1929, the garden was neglected for twenty-four years until Julius Fleischmann of Cincinnati, Ohio, acquired the gardens and surrounding land bringing the total to nearly two hundred acres. Fleischmann created two lakes on the grounds, put in strolling trails, and opened the park as Caribbean Gardens in 1954.

"When Mr. Fleischmann died, [the trustees] called my father in Ohio," said David. "He jumped at the chance to lease it. We'd had our contract at Cedar Point since 1964 and in the winter my father rented a barn in Medina, Ohio. The winter shows were productive and provided more than adequate income. The school shows were special for my dad. That's how he started—by lecturing in schools. But, he wanted a place where the animals could be outside in the sunshine all winter instead of in a heated barn. So we opened Jungle Larry's in September of 1969."

A.4 Florida Gov. Claude Kirk with Larry and tiglon cubs in October, 1969.

Before the Tetzlaffs took over the park it had only one animal show—Duck Vaudeville—that had appeared on many TV shows, including the Ed Sullivan show. In the act ducks played a piano, then slid into the water and tossed hoops. The show had a three-year life span and was up for renewal, costing about $30,000 for new birds. The Tetzlaffs, rather than put thousands of dollars into the duck act, presented their chimp, elephant, and big cat act. Renamed Jungle Larry's African Safari, the park presented mostly African animals—elephants, leopards, lions, and birds.

The park was losing money at the time of the change in owners. Larry offset the loss with income from his movies, as a double for Tarzan, and outside exhibits, making the park self-supporting by 1975. Larry felt he'd rather go under than ask for government funding; he felt strongly that private industry should succeed on its own. Today the park remains self-sustaining without local, state, or federal support.

As he improved the facility, Larry built a souvenir shop, offices and snack bar, and a sheltered animal arena for the audience. He bought three coach trains, decorated them with zebra stripes, and gave each tramful of forty-eight passengers a tour.

A.5 Jungle Larry and Safari Jane.

It is in this lush setting that the Tetzlaffs conserve endangered animal species, educate, and entertain the public.

For a decade after Larry's death, the Tetzlaffs retained the Jungle Larry's name to keep alive memories of their world-famous husband and father. Park visitors also remembered Jungle Larry and respected the park's tradition. However, on the park's fortieth anniversary, in 1994, to encompass future plans for the park, the name was officially changed back to Caribbean Gardens, Home of Jungle Larry's Zoological Park.

Educational Rides and Shows

Between animal shows, visitors can see the grounds via a twenty-five-minute tram ride. While traveling this winding pine-needle trail, the tram driver presents a lively overview of the entire park—its history, animals, and plants. In the "rain forest," the driver tells riders that almost all the trees in Jungle Larry's rain forest actually came from jungle forests. The trees in the Amazon, Indian, Indonesian, and Malaysian rain forests are so tall and dense that very little sunlight filters through to the ground. Fifty percent of the world's plants and animals came from the rain forest, but because man has destroyed so much of the rain forest, these plants and shrubs are quickly becoming irreplaceable.

After the ride, visitors can walk on the tram path while the sun reflects off the bright flowers. Many areas have trees, including those enclosed for the lions, monkeys, and tigers. Each climbing animal's space is covered with chain link and/or netting with metal roofs. The enclosures have sheltered areas to provide the animals with protection from heat and rain. The animals also have various toys for exercise and enjoyment, such as tires and balls for the big cats, stones for leopards to climb, and ladders for monkeys.

On the park's big Lake Victoria (named after the African lake), visitors can take the twenty-minute Safari Island Cruise. The catamaran's captain welcomes people aboard his craft and continues by showing them a myriad of plants on the eight islands. The individual islands are also home to animals of a single species, such as brown lemurs or ring-tailed lemurs. The islands are spaced so that their inhabitants cannot leap to the next one and so each species lives without cages in a natural habitat. Besides the many species of lemurs (brown, white front, ring-tail, black and white ruffed), visitors will also see a variety of monkey species including the colobus, patas, and spider, and white-handed gibbons (tail-less ape).

The captain enjoys telling his riders about the animals' natural behaviors and history. According to the captain's talk, by the late 1800s, hunters almost made the colobus monkey extinct because of the demand for its black and white pelt. In another story, the captain explains that European explorers visiting the island of Madagascar often saw lemurs' eyes reflecting their lights in the dark and thought they must be ghosts. Hence the name "lemur," which means ghost in Latin.

During the ride, visitors can see the animals playing, chasing each other through concrete tubes and through trees, and eating. The animals are well cared for in ways not readily apparent to visitors. Little huts on the islands are heated during the chilly winter nights and underground piping brings fresh water to these island inhabitants.

One of the regular acts at Caribbean Gardens, Animal Antics, an entertaining and educational presentation of small exotic animals and birds—is also part of Jungle Larry's educational tradition. The show is presented on an outdoor stage shaded by the feathery green leaves and hundreds of orange flowers of a forty-foot orange poinciana tree. Bleachers seating one hundred fifty people surround three sides of this stage. Three staff members, including David, bring out four or five small animals, such as a leashed caracal or colobus monkey, an unleashed hedgehog, iguana, and a snake, and talk about that animal's natural habitat, behaviors, eating habits, and so on. Some of the animals, such as the hedgehog, and iguana, are taken into the bleachers so members of the audience may touch them. Later, the bird show presents macaws, and African grey, and Amazon parrots talking and performing stunts, such as riding a bird-size bicycle.

A.6 Animal Antics show where the visitors can get close-up experience with smaller animals.

Jungle Larry's employees enjoy helping park visitors have fun. Grant Smith's words summarize this. "One day after my tram ride, a woman got off it smiling ear to ear and said to me 'That made my day!' That's why I work here. It's not just a job. It's pleasure, fun, and a privilege. I've never been this happy in my life, and I was quite happy editing Disney films for ten years. But this beats it. It really does."

Appendix B

A Brief History of Big Cat Training

Thirty or forty years ago people wanted a different kind of animal show in America. Similar to a bullfight of years ago, the audience wanted the trainer to go in the ring and look like he wasn't going to come out. —David Tetzlaff

LIONS HAVE BEEN trained for thousands of years. Tiger training started a few hundred years ago, though no animals were born in captivity and hand raised. After they were caught, the trainer would break the animals' wild spirit by force. This was not considered cruel, because people generally felt wild animals were not like us—they were not intelligent, had no feelings, and could not communicate.

In the nineteenth century, tigers, lions, leopards, elephants, and other animals were displayed in a traveling zoo called the circus menagerie. An American, Isaac Van Amburgh, created one of the first circus wild animal acts by getting into the cage with his animals. Some "animal tamers" in the late 1800s and early 1900s trained their animals to roar and strike out, as to simulate an attack. As Joanne Joys explained in *Wild Animal Trainer in America,* the trainer and animals became actors.

Early records describe Carl Hagenbeck, in 1891 "conquering" a great number of animals, using the unlikely combination of two tigers, two lions, two black panthers, two leopards, three angora goats, two sheep, an Indian dwarf zebu, a Shetland pony, and two poodles.

Other tales from the early 1900s were of Jack Bonavita presenting twenty-seven lions in one act and Louis Roth's later topping that record with his twenty-eight lions.

In the period from the 1930s to 1950s, some trainers stand out for their renowned style. Clyde Beatty is perhaps the most famous name in lion and tiger training. A movie was made from Beatty's biography, *The Big Cage*. Impressed with the strength and ferocity of lions and tigers, audiences were thrilled by acts where the man used his power and courage to subdue the wild animal by holding a wooden chair, cracking a horse whip on the cage floor, and firing a blank pistol. During his performances, Clyde Beatty often put his head in a lion's mouth. In 1932, Beatty set a record with thirty-eight tigers and lions in his act. Many trainers did not use males and females in the same act, in order to lessen the chance of cat fights. But Beatty's act used both sexes.

Pat White, who presents tigers for the Circus Yano in Japan, told me more about the history of animal training. "Training styles have progressed remarkably in the last thirty years. People used to enjoy the trainer 'conquering' the animal in the arena. With due respect to Clyde Beatty, one consummate showman, his training methods were really rough compared to how most people handle animals today. There was a lot of force and a lot of fear used."

This offensive imposition of man's will on an animal is typified in training as late as the 1940s and 1950s, when some trainers evidently used shock sticks (hand-held, battery-driven cattle prods) to shock the animal. Nancy told me that aside from being inhumane, this is counterproductive, because the angry animals will come right at a trainer.

In the 1940s, Alfred Court, a Frenchman, brought his act to America. Referring to his animals as "truly tame," he presented something Americans were not used to. He began the transition from animals performing out of fear to performing for enjoyment. Court was ahead of his time, however. Baumann, who came after Court, also taught through kindness, but many trainers still used harsh training methods.

In the 1970s, Baumann made history with several acts: A five-tiger rollover, ten-tiger sit-up, and two mirror-ball rolling tigers. Talking about this example of a classic trainer, David told me,

"After Baumann's biography [was published], he beat his own record by doing a seven-tiger rollover. Then later he did a thirteen-tiger sit-up. I've seen Gunther [Gebel-Williams, Ringling's big-cat trainer during the 1970s to 1980s] do fifteen or sixteen. I have pictures of Josip Marcan doing a seventeen-tiger sit-up [1980s]. Wade Burck (also Ringling's tiger trainer) has done an eight-tiger rollover. I've rolled over six leopards. Gunther did five or six leopards. If you took Charly Baumann's act in its heyday and put it now, it'd still be one of the best in the world."

While walking the path at Jungle Larry's, Nancy told me, "It was different in the 1930s when animals were broken [tamed] in three months using ropes and chains. Now training may take about a year, but the difference is obvious. When you see an act trained by force, their animals never take their eyes off the trainer. They're scared. When David is working his leopards their eyes wander. The cats aren't afraid to look at the audience."

Increased esteem for animals led to different attitudes about entertainment. Many people now want to see the animals' natural grace and behaviors that would occur in the jungle rather than the artificial "tricks" that were presented in the past eras. The audience expects the animals to be themselves and the trainer to have a more personal relationship with his charges. By having hand-raised animals, trainers have a close relationship with each animal he presents.

David's closeness to his animals looks so easy. He told me that the proximity actually puts him in more danger than that of the old-school trainers who had a chair, whip, and gun between himself and the animal. "The macho man dominating his wild animals is not a side of the business, the animal, or me that I want to bring out. Now I go in there and sit on a tiger, actually placing myself in more jeopardy than they did years ago because they didn't get that close to the animal. The closer you get, the less effort that particular cat has to make to get hold of you. Like when a leopard is on your neck, he doesn't have to get off his seat, jump, or anything. He's right there to get you. The same thing with sitting on a tiger's back. More than one trainer has done that and the tiger turned around and took a kneecap. I wonder how much the public realizes what you do to get a close relationship like that. It's more comfortable for the animal because they don't feel somebody's breathing down their neck, forcing them, making them act vicious. It's also better for me, when I know my animals are comfortable."

B.1   Best of friends.

Appendix C

Recommended Reading
* Especially recommended by David Tetzlaff

Books

* Baumann, Charly and Leonard A. Stevens. *Tiger, Tiger: My 25 Years with the Big Cats*. Chicago: Playboy Press, 1975.

Beatty, Clyde and Edward Anthony. *Facing the Big Cats*. Garden City, New York: Doubleday, 1965.

Beatty, Clyde and Edward Anthony. *The Big Cage*. New York: Century Company, 1933.

* Court, Alfred. *My Life with the Big Cats*. New York: Simon & Schuster, 1955.

Edey, Maitland. *The Cats of Africa*. New York: Time-Life Books, 1968.

* Gebel-Williams, Gunther and Toni Reinhold. *Untamed*. New York: Morrow, 1991.

* Hanna, Jack. *Monkeys on the Interstate*. New York: Doubleday, 1989.

Hediger, Dr. H. *Wild Animals in Captivity*. Translated by G. Sircom. New York: Dover Publications, 1964.

* Johnson, William. *The Rose-Tinted Menagerie*. London: Heretic Books, 1990.

* Joys, Joanne Carol. *Wild Animal Trainer in America*. Boulder, Colo.: Pruett Publishing Company. 1983.

Keller, George. *Here Keller, Train This*. New York: Random House, 1961.

* Kiley-Worthington, Marthe. *Animals in Circuses and Zoos: Chiron's World?* Basildon, Essex, England: Little Eco-Farms Publishing, 1990.

* Knight, Frank, Susan Lumpkin, and John Seidensticker. *Great Cats*. Emmaus, Penn.: Rodale Press, 1991.

Loxton, Howard. *Guide to the Cats of the World*. Secaucus, New Jersey: Chartwell Books, 1990.

Loxton, Howard. *The Noble Cat*. New York: Portland House, 1990.

* National Geographic. *Book of Mammals*. Washington, DC: National Geographic, 1981.

Singh, Arjan. *Tiger! Tiger!* London: Jonathan Cape, 1984.

Stark, Mabel. *Hold That Tiger*. Caldwell, Idaho: Caxton Printers, 1940.

Magazines

* Hall, Elizabeth. "Gunther Gebel-Williams, Lord of the Ring," *Psychology Today*. (October 1983): 26-32.

Reed, Susan and Carol Azizian. "No Escape Claws," *People*, (July 1, 1991): 79-81

"Tiger, Tiger, Fading Fast," *Time*, 28 March 1994, 44-51.

"Wade Burck," edited by Eric Levin. *People*, (July 8, 1985): 60-63.

About the Author

Sharon Rendell and Maya

S HARON RENDELL began her writing career at age nineteen on a Florida newspaper when she worked as a features writer.

A graduate of the University of Illinois, with a double major in social work and psychology, and a minor in English, she was one semester short of a master's degree in social work when she decided to pursue her main interest—writing. She gained valuable experience as a college-text proofreader for Williams & Wilkins and Prentice Hall. Ms. Rendell has done technical writing for several companies, including Gould Computer Systems. She has written or co-authored twenty-three computer software manuals and has edited award-winning journal articles.

She was commissioned by the International Zoological Society to write this informative and personal account of the people and history of Jungle Larry's.

Ms. Rendell enjoys music and butterfly gardening, and reads voraciously. She lives in Urbana, Illinois with her family and two cats, where she is working on her next book.

To order additional copies of:

Living with
Big Cats

The Story of Jungle Larry,
Safari Jane,
and
David Tetzlaff

by Sharon Rendell

Send a copy of this page with $11.95 (U.S.), $14.95 (Canada) per copy, plus 6 % sales tax for Florida residents.

Please include $3.50 shipping and handling first book—$1.50 shipping and handling for each additional book.

Please send _____ copy(ies) to:

Name _____

Address _____

City _____ State _____ Zip _____

Phone_____

Payment by: ☐ Check   ☐ Visa   ☐ Mastercard

Card # _____ Expiration Date _____

Signature Required_____

Date_____

Mail to: **International Zoological Society**
1708 San Bernardino Way
Naples, FL 33942-7129